Easy Start Mandarin Chinese

总策划 屈哨兵
总主编 余广大

汉语1234

（汉英对照）

主　编 刘惠琼
副主编 陈荷荣
编　者 贾红霞　何嘉玲　黄　梦　蒋洪文
李静娜　李　爽　梁　曼　卢梓筠
祁　辉

First Edition 2014

ISBN 978-7-119-07357-6

Published by Foreign Languages Press Co. Ltd
24 Baiwanzhuang Road, Beijing 100037, China
http://www.flp.com.cn E-mail: flp@cipg.org.cn
Distributed by China International Book Trading Corporation
35 Chegongzhuang Xilu, Beijing 100044, China
P.O. Box 399, Beijing, China
Printed in the People's Republic of China

目　录
Contents

说　明
Instruction

《汉语1234》是“轻松开始学汉语”丛书中的一本，阅读对象是以汉语为第二语言的人，目的在于为学习者理解和运用会话中的基本语句提供一种支持。本书简短、实用，特点如下：

This book, compiled for CSL readers, is one of *Easy Start Mandarin Chinese.* To help the readers to better understand and apply more easily the basic Chinese sentence patterns provided in this book, the compilers have attached to each of them a brief explanation as well as a practical dialogue. This book is characterized with the following advantages.

1. 句子简短
Short, simple and practical dialogues

日常生活各种场景中，长度在4个音节之内的首个话轮，是本书筛选句子的一个原则。这里的首个话轮实际上就是一次会话过程中，听话者听到发话者发出的长度在4个音节之内的第一句话。即收集的分别是1个音节、2个音节、3个音节和4个音节的第一句话。例如：

It is a general principle that the sentence starting each dialogue must be within 4 syllables, which are all used frequently in everyday life. That is, the person who starts each dialogue just use simple, short and practical sentences no more than 4 syllables in the first round. Therefore, the first sentences collected in the starting round of each dialogue in this book are respectively one syllable sentences, two syllable sentences, three syllable sentences and four syllable sentences. This can be well illustrated by the following 2 examples.

例一：

林　海：哎。
丁小宁：怎么了?
林　海：他怎么来了?
这段会话中的首个话轮为一个音节构成的一句话“哎”。

Example One

Lin Hai：Hey!
Ding Xiaoning: What's the matter?
Lin Hai：Why has he come?
It is“哎”, a one syllable sentence that starts the first round of this dialogue.

例二：

老师：把书给我。
丁小宁：好的，给您书。

这段会话的首个话轮为四个音节构成的一句话。

Example Two

Teacher: Pass me the book, please.

Ding Xiaoning: Ok. Here you are.

It is “把书给我”, a four syllable sentence that starts the first round of this dialogue.

2. 场景多样
Various types of settings /contexts

本书语料来源于日常生活及对外汉语会话教材。会话场景的涉及面较广，涉及到学习、购物、旅游等日常生活的多方面。

Before compiling this book, the chief compiler had read a lot of CSL textbooks of this type popular both at home and abroad and then she sorted out the most useful materials for reference. This explains why the sentence patterns and the dialogues selected in this book involve various aspects of life, namely campus life, shopping, travelling and so on. As they are all based on everyday life experiences of average Chinese people, this book, being practical and useful, can also provide the readers with rich knowledge of Chinese culture.

3. 适用范围广
Wide applicability

本书既可作为初学汉语的人会话学习的帮手，也可作为有一定汉语基础的人在听话过程中遇到理解困难时的参考。

The book can satisfy various demands of different readers for its large coverage of all kinds of topics. For the beginners, this book can help them to acquire more basic Chinese sentence patterns which they will find to be very useful & practical in everyday conversation; for those who have learned some Chinese, it may serve as a reference book when they encounter difficulties in listening to or interpreting contents of various topscs.

4. 查找运用方便
Great convenience in checking and practice

本书按音节数分类，同类中再按音序顺序排列，便于使用者查找。如果学习者在生活中听到发话者的第一个句子（1~4个音节的句子）的音节数及句子的第一个音，那么就可

说　明
Instruction

能在这本小册子中找到相应的句子，使用较为方便。例如：你听到的第一句话是“别嘟囔了。”4个音节，第一个音节是bie，你就可以在《音节表》中“四个音节的句子”类的bie音节处找到句子所处的位置（P196）然后找到该句。

The sentence patterns in this book are generally compiled according to the number of syllables each of them contains, under which they are arranged in accordance with the alphabetical order of the initial sound of the initial syllable of each sentence. Therefore, it is convenient for the learners to check and practice any sentence they are looking for. For instance, if a learner has heard the first sentence of a dialogue, he/she can find out that sentence in this book just according to the number of the syllables that sentence contains and the initial sound of its initial syllable. For example, if the first sentence one has heard in a dialogue is “别嘟囔了”, one just check the part of the book that covers 4 syllable sentences. As the initial sound of its initial syllable in this sentence is “bie” (别), one can soon find this sentence under the category of “B”.

本书在每一个句子的下面分列有句子的英文

翻译、句义解释和语句运用，力求使用者能够在查到句子后不仅能知晓句子的意思，还能在一定的语境中运用。例如:

To help the readers understand the sentence patterns, each Chinese sentence has been supplied with an English equivalent. Instructions and examples in both Chinese and English are provided to each of them so that the readers can know clearly not only their meaning but also their usage. The following is an example.

贵　姓?
询问对方姓氏的敬语。
Used to inquire about one’s family name.
小　刘：贵姓?
　　　　Guìxìng?
张先生：免贵姓张。
　　　　Miǎn guì xìng Zhāng.
Xiao Liu：Your surname, please?
Mr.Zhang：Zhang.

为了学习者的方便，会话中人物的身份及关系在本书中也有一个大致的区分：简萍、甘玲、林海、丁小宁为大学同班同学；小刘和小韩为公司的同事；黄小姐和徐小姐为朋友；陈教授和白老师为大学同事；约翰和杰克为大学留学生。其他在会话中有身份标示的人物在这里就不再说明。

In order to make the learners understand the dialogues more easily, the relationship between the participants in the dialogues have been specified as follows: Jian Ping, Gan Ling ,Lin Hai and Ding Xiaoning are classmates at college; Xiao Liu and Xiao Han are colleagues in a company; Miss Huang and Miss Xu are friends; Professor Chen and Teacher Bai are colleagues in a university; John and Jack are foreign students studying Chinese in a university. There will be no more explanation about those whose identities have been specified in the dialogues of this book.

本书编撰过程中，教材资料的查找得到中山大学国际汉语教材研发与培训基地的支持。另外，有些词语的解释参考了《现代汉语词典》（商务印书馆2002年版）和《现代汉语规范词典》（外语教学与研究出版社、语文出版社2004年版）的相关释义。在此，本书编者一并致谢。

The compilers of this book would like to express our sincere gratitude to all those who have offered various help to make this book better and more useful. Our thanks should also be expressed to CSL Textbook Developing and Training Center of Sun Yat-sen University, which opened their library to the chief compiler to search for relevant material. Besides, we'd like to express our heartfelt thanks to *Modern Chinese Dictionary* (published by *Commercial Press* in 2002) and 2 versions of *Modern Chinese Standard Dictionary* (published respectively by *Foreign language Teaching and Research Press* and *China Language Press* in 2004), which provide much useful information for the compilers in defining difficult words they encounter. Without them this book may not come into being as planned.

A 1 哎。Āi.

Hey.

① 表示惊讶。

Used to express one's surprise.

林　海：哎。
　　　　Āi.
丁小宁：怎么了?
　　　　Zěnme le?
林　海：他怎么来了?
　　　　Tā zěnme lái le?

Lin Hai: Hey!
Ding Xiaoning: What's the matter?
Lin Hai: Why has he come?

② 呼唤、提醒对方注意。

Used to call one's attention.

老板：哎。
　　　Āi.
职员：啊?
　　　Ā?
老板：你，就是你来一下。
　　　Nǐ, jiù shì nǐ lái yī xià.

Boss: Hey!
Employee: Yes?
Boss: you, come here please!

A 2 哎！Ái!

Gosh!

① 表示诧异。

Used to express one's surprise.

小韩：哎！
Ái!

小刘：怎么了？
Zěnme le?

小韩：怎么是他？
Zěnme shì tā?

Xiao Han: Gosh!
Xiao Liu: What's the matter?
Xiao Han: How can it be him?

② 突然想起什么要告诉对方。

Used to tell somebody something that suddenly occurs to the speaker.

小韩：哎！
Ái!

小刘：怎么了？
Zěnme le?

小韩：差点儿忘了告诉你，科长要你明天去总部开会。
Chàdiǎnr wàngle gàosu nǐ, kēzhǎng yào nǐ míngtiān qù zǒngbù kāihuì.

Xiao Han: Whoops
Xiao Liu: What's the matter?
Xiao Han: I almost forget to tell you one thing. Our section chief asks you to attend a meeting at the headquarters tomorrow.

A 3 唉。Ài.

Sigh!

① 表示伤感、失望。

Used to express one's regret or disappointment.

孩子：唉。
Ài.
父亲：怎么了？比赛输了？
Zěnme le? bǐsài shū le?
孩子：嗯，输了。
Ǹ, shū le.
Children: Sigh!
Father: What's wrong with you? Lost the game?
Children: Yeah. we Lost the game.

② 表示惋惜、懊悔。

Used to express one's regret or pity.

小韩：唉。

Ài.

小刘：怎么了？

Zěnme le?

小韩：这么好的机会又错过了。

Zhème hǎo de jīhuì yòu cuòguò le.

小刘：别唉声叹气的，以后还有机会。

Bié āishēng-tànqì de, yǐhòu hái yǒu jīhuì.

Xiao Han: Alas!
Xiao Liu: What happened?
Xiao Han: I have missed another good opportunity.
Xiao Liu: Do not moan and groan. You will have other opportunities.

B 1 爸。Bà.

Dad

呼喊父亲。

Used to call one's dad.

C 1　车。Chē.

A general term referring to cars, buses, trucks, trains & the like.

① 告诉对方车来了,准备上车，或有车来，注意安全。

To remind somebody that a car, bus, truck or a train is coming, so he/she should get ready to get on it; To warn somebody against an approaching vehicle.

小韩：车。
　　Chē.
小刘：车来了?
　　Chē lái le?
小韩：是啊。
　　Shì ā.
小刘：我们准备上车吧。
　　Wǒmen zhǔnbèi shàngchē ba.

Xiao Han: The car/bus /train is coming.
Xiao Liu: Really?
Xiao Han: Yeah.
Xiao Liu: Let's get ready to get on the car/bus /train now.

② 招呼、示意出租车过来载客，表示自己需要乘车。

Used to call a taxi.

乘客：车。
Chē.

出租车司机：你好，去哪里?
Nǐ hǎo , qù nǎli?

乘客：去机场。
Qù jīchǎng.

Passengers: Taxi .
Taxi driver: Hello! Where to go?
Passengers: The airport, please.

G 1　哥。Gē.

Elder brother.

① 称呼同父母（或只同父、只同母）年龄比自己大的男性。

② 称呼同辈中年龄比自己大的男性。

③ 称呼跟自己年龄差不多的男性，是一种敬称。

Used to call one's elder brother or a male cousin who is older than oneself; Used as an honorific form to call a male of similar age so as to show one's respect.

G 2 乖。Guāi.

Be a good boy/girl!

① 要小孩听话，别淘气，一般为成人对小孩儿说。

Used to ask small children (usually one's son or daughter) to be obedient or not to be naughty.

妈妈：乖。
Guāi.

孩子：不嘛，太苦了，我不吃。
Bù ma , tài kǔ le , wǒ bù chī.

妈妈：宝宝乖，吃了药，肚子就不痛了。
Bǎobao guāi , chīle yào , dùzi jiù bùtòng le.

Mom: Be a good boy/girl! Take the medicine.

Child: No, I won't have it. It's too bitter to take.
Mom: Good boy/girl. Take the medicine and you will have no stomachache.

② 赞扬小孩儿机灵、听话。

Used to praise a child who is smart and obedient.

妈妈：乖。
Guāi.
宝宝：妈妈。
Māma.
妈妈：宝宝真乖，自己把饭吃完了，没让妈妈喂。
Bǎobao zhēn guāi, zìjǐ bǎ fàn chī wán le , méi ràng māma wèi.

Mom: Good boy/girl.
Baby: Mom.
Mom: Good boy/girl. You have had the meal without asking mummy to feed you.

G 3　滚！ Gǔn!

Go away!

让对方离开，一般用于斥责、辱骂对方。

Used to reprimand someone or order someone to leave the place.

女朋友：滚！
Gǔn!

男朋友：有话好好儿说，别这样。一定有什么误会，你听我解释。
Yǒu huà hǎohǎor shuō , bié zhèyàng. yīdìng yǒu shénme wùhuì, nǐ tīng wǒ jiěshì.

女朋友：让你滚，你就滚。我再也不想见到你！
Ràng nǐ gǔn, nǐ jiù gǔn . wǒ zài yě bù xiǎng jiàndào nǐ!

Girlfriend: Go away!

Boyfriend: Don't behave like that. There must be a misunderstanding between us. You should listen to my explanation.

Girlfriend: Go away! I let you go away! I don't want to see you anymore!

H 1 咳。Hāi.

Hi.

向对方打招呼或提醒。

Used to greet someone or call one's attention.

小韩：咳。
Hāi.
小刘：咳，你好！
Hāi, nǐ hǎo!

Xiao Han: Hi.
Xiao Liu: Hi, Good morning/afternoon/evening!

H 2 嗨。Hēi.

Hello/ hi/oh, oh/Alas.

① 向对方打招呼。

Used to greet someone or call one's attention.

小韩：嗨。
Hēi.
小刘：嗨，你好！
Hēi, nǐ hǎo!

Xiao Han: Hi.
Xiao Liu: Hi, Good morning/afternoon/ evening!

② 表示惊异。

Used to show one's surprise.

小韩：嗨。
Hēi.
小刘：怎么了?
Zěnme le!
小韩：我的手机怎么不见了。
Wǒ de shǒujī zěnme bù jiàn le.

Xiao Han: Oh, oh!
Xiao Liu: What's the matter?
Xiao Han: I can't find my cell phone.

③ 表示惋惜,感慨或责怪。

Used to express one's pity or regret.

小韩：嗨。
Hēi.
小刘：还在为上午的事自责吗?
Hái zài wèi shàngwǔ de shì zìzé ma?
小韩：我要是再劝劝，他也许就不会辞职了。真可惜!
Wǒ yàoshì zài quànquan, tā yěxǔ jiù bù huì cízhí le. Zhēn kěxī!

Xiao Han: Alas
Xiao Liu: still blame yourself for what happened in the morning?
Xiao Han: If I had tried harder to persuade him, probably he would not have resigned. What a pity!

J 1 姐。Jiě.

Sister.

① 称呼同父母（或只同父、只同母）而比自己年纪大的女子。

② 称呼同辈中年龄比自己大的女性。

③ 称呼跟自己年龄差不多的女性，是一种敬称。

Used to call one's elder sister or a female cousin who is older than oneself; Used as an honorific term to call a female of similar age so as to show one's respect.

K 1 看。Kàn.

Look。

叫对方注意某种情况。

Used to call someone to pay attention to something.

邻居甲：看。
Kàn.

邻居乙：好大的烟啊！火灾?
Hǎo dà de yān Ā! Huǒzāi?

邻居甲：应该是火灾，我们赶紧报警!
Yīnggāi shì huǒzāi, wǒmen gǎnjǐn bàojǐng!

Neighbor A: Look.
Neighbor B: What a big smoke! Is there a fire accident?
Neighbor A: I think so. Let's dial fire telephone!

L 1 来。Lái.

Come here.

叫对方过来。

Used to call someone to come up to

the speaker himself.

小韩：来。
Lái.

小刘：好，来了。
Hǎo, lái le.

Xiao Han: Come here!
Xiao Liu: Ok. Here I am.

M 1 妈。Mā.

Mum.

呼喊母亲。

Used to call one's mum.

M 2 慢！Màn!

Just a moment/Stop!/ Whoa!

让对方的行动停下来。

Used to stop someone from doing something.

小韩：慢！
Màn!
小刘：怎么了？
Zěnme le?
小韩：她不能再喝了，这杯酒我帮她喝了。
Tā bù néng zài hē le, zhè bēi jiǔ wǒ bāng tā hē le.

Xiao Han: Just a moment!
Xiao Liu: What's the matter?
Xiao Han: She has drunk too much. I drink this glass of alcohol for her.

N 1 喏。Nuò.

Hey!

让对方注意自己所指示的事物。

Used to call someone to pay attention to what is being indicated .

林海：喏。
Nuò.
丁小宁：什么？
Shénme?
林海：你看，黑板上又有新的通知。
Nǐ kàn, hēibǎn shàng yòu yǒu xīn de tōngzhī.

Lin Hai: Hey.
Ding Xiaoning: Yes?
Lin Hai: Look! There is a new notice on the blackboard.

Q 1 瞧。Qiáo.

Look.

让对方看自己所指示的事物。

Used to call someone to look at what is being indicated.

简萍：瞧。
Qiáo.

甘玲：什么？
Shén me?

简萍：那儿有只蝴蝶。
Nàr yǒu zhī húdié.

甘玲：真漂亮！
Zhēn piāoliang!

Jian Ping: Look.
Gan Ling: What?
Jian Ping: There is a butterfly over there.
Gan Ling: Wow, how beautiful it is!

S 1 谁？Shéi?

Who is it?

询问对方身份，多用在询问屋外敲门的人是什么人。

Often used to inquire who is knocking at the door.

小韩：谁?
Shéi?
小刘：我，小刘。你开开门。
Wǒ, Xiǎo Liú. Nǐ kāikai mén.

JXiao Han: Who is it?
Xiao Liu: It's me, Liu. Open the door, please.

T 1 疼。Téng.

Ouch/Ow.

由于疼痛，忍不住地叫出声。

Used as a way of groaning because of sharp pain.

女儿：疼。
Téng.
妈妈：哪里疼?
Nǎli téng?
女儿：肚子。
Dùzi.

Daughter: Ouch.
Mum: Where does it ache?
Daughter: stomach.

T 2 听。Tīng.

Listen!

提醒对方听声音。

Used to ask someone to listen to some sound.

小韩：听。
Tīng.

小刘：什么?
Shén me?

小韩：好像有人在叫我们。
Hǎo xiàng yǒu rén zài jiào wǒmen.

小刘：是的，小蒋在叫我们呢，我们赶紧去吧。
Shì de, Xiǎo Jiǎng zài jiào wǒmen ne, wǒmen gǎnjǐn qù ba.

Xiao Han: listen.
Xiao Liu: What?
Xiao Han: It seems there is someone calling us.
Xiao Liu: Yes, Xiao Jiang is calling us. Let's go.

W 1 喂。Wèi.

Hello.

打招呼，有要求对方作出回应的意思，常用在电话通话开始时，或提醒对方。

Used to greet somebody and wait for his or her response, especially in making a phone call or used to remind someone of something.

小韩：喂。
Wèi.

小刘：喂。你好，小韩吗?
Wèi. Nǐ hǎo, Xiǎo Hán ma?

小韩：是。
Shì.

Xiao Han: Hello.
Liu: Hello! Is Xiao Han speaking?
Xiao Han: Yes.

Y 1 呀！Ya！

Dear me/Oh, my/ My goodness!

表示惊疑。

Used to show one's surprise.

小韩：呀！
Ya！

小刘：又怎么了？一惊一乍的！
Yòu zěnme le！Yījīng yīzhà de！

小韩：糟糕！钥匙忘在家里了。
Zāogāo！Yàoshi wàng zài jiālǐ le.

Xiao Han: Dear me!
Liu: What's wrong? What makes you so upset?
Xiao Han: My goodness! I've locked the key in the house.

Y 2 咦！Yí！

Ah/ Oh, oh!/ Aha

① 表示惊讶。

Used to express one's surprise with rising tone.

小韩：咦！
Yí!
小刘：怎么了？
Zěnme le?
小韩：我的钱包呢，怎么找不到了？
Wǒ de qiánbāo ne , zěnme zhǎo bù dào le?

Xiao Han: Oh, oh!
Xiao Liu: What's the matter?
Xiao Han: Where is my wallet? I can't find it.

② 表示嘲讽、鄙夷。

Used to show one's contempt or mockery.

小韩：咦！
Yí!
小刘：怎么了？
Zěnme le?
小韩：他也能获奖？真是太阳从西边出来了！
Tā yě néng huòjiǎng? Zhēnshi tàiyang cóng xībian chūlái le!
小刘：你呀，别太小看人家了。
Nǐ ya, bié tài xiǎokàn rénjia le.

Xiao Han: Aha!
Xiao Liu: What's up?
Xiao Han: He can win a prize? Once in a blue moon!
Xiao Liu: You shouldn't look down upon him.

Y 3 呦。Yōu.

Oh, my!

① 表示惊异。

Used to show one's surprise.

林　海：呦。
Yōu.

丁小宁："呦"什么?
" Yōu " shénme?

林　海：今天是个什么特别的日子呀?教室里布置得这么漂亮!
Jīntiān shì gè shénme tèbié de rìzi ya? Jiàoshì li bùzhì de zhème piàoliàng!

丁小宁：有几个同学过生日。
Yǒu jǐ gè tóngxué guò shēngrì.

Lin Hai: Oh, my!
Ding Xiaoning: Why are you surprised?
Lin Hai: What special day is it today? The classroom is decorated so beautiful!
Ding Xiaoning: Today is the birthday of several classmates.

② 表示突然发现或想起。

Used to show something occurs to the speaker suddenly.

林　海：呦！
　　　　Yōu.
丁小宁：怎么了？
　　　　Zěnme le?
林　海：差点儿忘了，下午还要去看个同学。
　　　　Chàdiǎnr wàng le, xiàwǔ háiyào qù kàn gè tóngxué.

Lin Hai: Whoops!
Ding Xiaoning: What's the matter?
Lin Hai: I will go to meet a friend this afternoon. I almost forget it.

Z 1　早。Zǎo.

Morning!

早上见面时的问候语，同"早安"。

Used to greet each other in the morning.

A 1 哎呀。Āiyā.

My goodness/Good heavens!

① 表示惊讶。

Used to show one's shock or fear.

儿子：哎呀。
Āiya.
爸爸：怎么了?
Zěnme le?
儿子：不好了，爷爷的心脏病又发作了!
Bù hǎo le, yéye de xīnzāngbìng yòu fāzuò le!

Son: My goodness!
Dad: What's wrong?
Son: (Good) Heavens!, Grandpa had another heart attack!

② 表示痛苦。

Used to show one' s pain.

简萍：哎呀。
Āiya.
甘玲：脚还在疼吗?
Jiǎo hái zài téng ma?
简萍：是啊，昨天摔了一跤，今天不光是疼，还肿了。
Shì a, zuótiān shuāile yī jiào, jīntiān bù guāng shì téng, hái zhǒng le.

Jian Ping: Oh oh.
Gan Ling: Your feet still hurt?
Jian Ping: Yes, I fell and broke my ankle yesterday. Today it got swollen and more painful.

③ 表示着急。

Used to show one's anxiety.

陈教授：哎呀。
Āiya.

白老师：您怎么了？
Nín zěnme le?

陈教授：我三点要到广州大学开会，现在都快三点了，车还没有来，真急人。
Wǒ sān diǎn yào dào Guǎngzhōu Dàxué kāihuì, xiànzài dōu kuài sān diǎn le, chē hái méiyǒu lái, zhēn jí rén.

白老师：我去叫辆出租。
wǒ qù jiào liàng chūzū.

陈教授：好，谢谢。
Hǎo, xièxie.

Professor Chen: My God.
Teacher Bai: What's wrong?
Professor Chen: I'll have a meeting at three o'clock in Guangzhou University. It is almost three o'clock now, but the car has not come yet. What can I do?

Teacher Bai: I go and call a taxi for you.
Professor Chen: Fine, thank you.

A 2 安静！Ānjìng！

Quiet, please!

让大家停止喧哗和吵闹。

Used to ask people to stop making noise.

班长：安静！
Ānjìng！
简萍：静一静，大家都别吵啦！班长有事宣布。
Jìng yī jìng, dàjiā dōu bié chǎo la! bānzhǎng yǒu shì xuānbù.

Monitor: Quiet, please!
Jian Ping: Be quiet, everyone! Lend your ears to our monitor. He has something to announce .

A 3 按住。Ànzhù.

Press it.

叫对方用手或手指压住某物。

Used to ask someone to press something with one's finger or hand.

护士：按住。
Àn zhù.
病人：好的。要按多久?
Hǎo de. Yào àn duōjiǔ?.
护士：大约五分钟就可以了。
Dàyuē wǔ fēnzhōng jiù kěyǐ le.

Nurse: Press it.
Patient: Yes. How many minutes?
Nurse: About 5 minutes.

B 1 爸爸。Bàba.

Daddy

呼喊父亲。同“爸”。

Used to call one's father with the same meaning as '爸'

B 2 拜拜。Bàibai.

Bye-bye.

告别时的礼貌用语，语气较为随意。

Used as an informal way to say goodbye.

B 3 饱了。Bǎo le.

I'm full.

表示自己吃足了，已经满足食量。

Used to show one is full and cannot eat any more.

女儿：饱了。
Bǎo le.

妈妈：不再吃点儿？
Bù zài chīdiǎnr?

女儿：不了，再吃就撑了。
Bù le, zài chī jiù chēng le.

Daughter: I'm full.
Mother: Won't you have more?
Daughter: Thank you. I'm too full to have any more.

B 4 表哥。Biǎo gē.

Cousin

称呼父亲的姐妹和母亲的兄弟姐妹的儿子中比自己年长的人。

Used to call the son of one's father' s sister or the son of one' s mother' s sister of brother, who is older than the speaker himself/herself.

B 5 表姐。Biǎo jiě.

Cousin

称呼父亲的姐妹、母亲的兄弟姐妹的女儿中比自己年长的人。

Used to call the daughter of one's' s sister of the daughter of one' s mother' s sister of brother. who is older than the speaker himself/ herself.

B 6 伯伯。Bóbo.

Uncle

称呼父亲的姐妹和母亲的兄弟姐妹的女儿中比自己年长的人。

Used to call the daughter of one's aunt or uncle, who is older than the speaker himself/herself.

① 称呼父亲的哥哥。

Used when refer to farher's elder brother.

② 称呼与父亲辈分相同，而年纪经父亲在的男子。

Used when refer to men who are older than one's father.

B 7 伯母。Bómǔ.

Aunt

称呼伯伯的妻子。

Used to call the wife of one's father's elder brother.

C 1 馋了？Chán le?

Mouth watered?

询问是不是想吃摆在面前的食物，通常带有玩笑亲近的意味。

Used to inquire if someone wants to eat the food in front of him/her often with a sense of joking or intimacy.

小韩：馋了？
Chán le?

小刘：是啊，这么香的红烧肉。
Shì a, zhème xiāng de hóngshāo ròu.

小韩：那就吃呗，还客气什么。
Nà jiù chī bei, hái kèqi shénme.

Xiao Han: Mouth watered?
Xiao Liu: Yeah. The pork smells so inviting that no one can resist it.
Xiao Han: Then what are you waiting for? Just take it.

C 2 尝尝。Chángchang.

Have a taste

① 请别人试吃/喝某种食物/饮品。

To ask someone to try some food or drink.

妻子：尝尝。
Chángchang.
丈夫：嗯，很好吃。
Ǹ, hěn hǎo chī.

Wife: Have a taste.
Husband: Mmmm! Yummy/Very delicious.

一个音节的句子 One-syllable Sentences
两个音节的句子 Two-syllable Sentences
三个音节的句子 Three-syllable Sentences
四个音节的句子 Four-syllable Sentences

② 请对方辨别滋味。

Used to ask someone to taste the food to see whether there is enough salt.

妻子：尝尝。
Chángchang.

丈夫：嗯，好像淡了点儿，再加点儿盐吧。
Ǹ, hǎo xiàng dànlediǎnr, zài jiādiǎr yán ba.

妻子：好。
Hǎo.

Wife: Have a taste.
Husband: Well, it seems not tasty enough. add a little salt to it.
Wife: Ok.

C 3 存钱。Cún qián.

I want to deposit some money.

告诉银行业务员自己要把钱存进银行。

To tell the clerk that one wants to deposit some money in the bank.

小　刘：存钱。
Cún qián.
业务员：好的。
Hǎode.
（小刘将人民币递给业务员。）
(Xlǎo Liú jiāng rénmínbì dìgěi yèwùyuán.)
业务员：您存多少钱?
Nín cún duōshao qián?
小　刘：2000。
2000.

Xiao Liu: I want to deposit some money.
Clerk: Okay.
(Xiao Liu handed the money to the clerk.)
Clerk: How much do you deposit?
Xiao Liu: 2000RMB.

D 1 打劫！ Dǎjié！

Robbery!

① 表示要抢东西了，一般是打劫者为了让被劫者放弃反抗喊出的恐吓人的话语。
Used to by the robbers to threaten those who will be robbed not to resist.

打劫者：打劫！
Dǎjié!
被劫者：快来人啊！有人打劫！
Kuài lái rén a! Yǒu rén dǎjié!

Robber: robbery!
Passerby: Help! Help! There are robbers here!

② 看到有人拦路抢夺财物或自己遭遇拦路抢夺财物时的呼救语。

Used by the robbed or passersby who witnesses the robbery to cry for help.

林　海：打劫！
Dǎjié!
丁小宁：我们赶紧过去抓住他！
Wǒmen gǎnjǐn guòqu zhuāzhu tā!

Lin Hai: Robbery!
Ding Xiaoning: Let's go to catch the robber.

D 2 当心。Dāngxīn.

Watch out/Look out.

提醒对方注意，留心。

Used to warn someone against the possible danger.

简萍：当心。
Dāngxīn.

甘玲：知道了。
Zhīdao le.

简萍：当心地滑，别摔着。
Dāngxīn dìhuá , bié shuāizhe.

甘玲：谢谢。
Xièxiè.

Jian Ping: Mind your steps.
Gan Ling: Thanks.
Jian Ping: Mind your steps. The floor is slippery.
Gan Ling: Thanks a lot.

D 3 等等。Děngdeng.

Wait for me, please.

叫对方等一下儿。

Used to ask someone to wait for the speaker himself.

简萍：等等。
Děngdeng.

甘玲：你怎么那么慢啊?
Nǐ zěnme nàme màn a?

简萍：太累了，我走不动了。
Tai lèi le, wǒ zǒubudòng le.

甘玲：那就休息一会儿吧。
Nàjiù xiūxī yīhuìér bā.

Jian Ping: Wait for me, please.
Gan Ling: Why do you walk so slowly?
Jian Ping: I am too tired to walk.
Gan Ling: Let's have a rest then.

D 4 第几？ Dì jǐ?

What place did he/they get?

一般询问比赛中某人或某个队的比赛名次。
Used to ask about the result of a match which someone has participated.

丁小宁：第几？
Dì jǐ?
林　海：第一！林丹现在排第一。
Dì–yī！ Lín Dān xiànzài pái dì–yī.

Ding Xiaoning: What place did Lin Dan get?
Lin Hai: First! Lin Dan is now ranked first.

D 5

点菜。
Diàn cǎi.

Please take my order/Where is the menu, please?

自己要指定菜式了，请服务员来记录。一般用在餐馆、酒店等用餐场合。

Used in restaurants, hotel or other places by the customers who ask waiter/waitress to take down their order for dinner.

徐小姐：点菜。
Diǎn cài.

服务员：请问您点些什么？
Qǐng wèn nín diǎn xiē shénme?

徐小姐：水煮鱼、麻婆豆腐……
Shuǐzhǔyú、mápó dòufu……

Miss Xu: Please take my order/ Please order for me.

Waiter/Waitress: What do you want to order, please?

Miss Xu: Spicy fish，Mapo tofu……

D 6 多重? Duō zhòng?

How heavy?

询问物体的重量。

Used to ask about the weight of something.

林　海：多重?
　　　　Duō zhòng?

丁小宁：一个西瓜三斤半。
　　　　Yī gè xīguā sān jīn bàn.

Lin Hai: How heavy?

Ding Xiaoning: This water-melon is three jin & half.

E 1 恶心。Ěxin.

Vomit

① 表示胃不舒服，想要呕吐。

Used to mean one is going to vomit.

林　海：恶心。
　　　　Ěxīn.

丁小宁：要吐吗?
　　　　Yào tù ma?

林　海：是，有些反胃。
Shì, yǒuxiē fǎnwèi.
Lin Hai: I am going to vomit.
Ding Xiaoning: Is it serious?
Lin Hai:Yes. It seems to be so.

② 表示极其讨厌。

Used to mean one is sick of something.

甘玲：恶心。
Ěxīn.
简萍：太恶心了，随地吐痰。
Tài ěxīn le , suídì tǔtán.
甘玲：他有没有点儿公德心啊。
Tā yǒu méiyǒudiǎnr gōngdéxīn a.
Gan Ling: Disgusting!
Jian Ping: Spit on the floor. How disgusting!
Gan Ling: Isn't he a citizen of some social morality?

E 2 饿了。È le.

I am hungry.

肚子没有食物，表示需要吃东西了。

Used to mean one is hungry and need to eat something.

女儿：饿了。
È le.
妈妈：还有一会儿才能吃饭，要不先吃点儿点心？
Háiyǒu yīhuìr cái néng chīfàn, yàobu xiān chīdiǎnr diǎnxīn?
女儿：好的。
Hǎo de.

Daughter: I am hungry, mum.
Mum: The food can't be ready in several minutes. Do you want some deserts?
Daughter: All right.

F 1 烦人！ Fánrén!

How annoying!

表示使人心烦。

Used to mean one is annoyed.

林 海：烦人！
Fánrén!
丁小宁：怎么了？
Zěnme le?
林 海：每天都收到垃圾短信。
Měitiān dōu shōudào hěnduō lājī duǎnxìn.

Lin Hai: How annoying!
Ding Xiaoning: What's up?
Lin Hai: Every day I receive a lot of spam messages.

G 1 干杯。Gānbēi.

Cheers!

劝对方把杯中的酒喝完，一般用在劝酒、祝酒的场合。

Used to propose a toast.

G 2 干了。Gān le.

It has dried up.

① 没有水分或水分少。

Used to mean something is dried or lack of water.

甘玲：干了。
Gān le.

简萍：这么快就干了。
Zhème kuài jiù gān le.

甘玲：是啊，秋天干燥，衣服容易干。
Shì a, qiūtiān gànzào, yīfu róngyi gān.

Gan Ling: The clothes have dried!
Jian Ping: The clothes dry so quickly!
Gan Ling: The fall is a dry season, so clothes can dry easily.

② 劝对方喝完杯中的酒。

Used to persuade someone to drink up the wine in the glass.

主人：干了。
Gān le.
客人：好，干了。
Hǎo, gān le.

Host: Bottoms up/Cheers!
Guest: Bottoms up/Cheers!

G 3 干吗？ Gàn má?

What for?

询问对方意图。

Used to ask what one's intention is.

儿子：干吗?
Gànmá?
妈妈：不干吗，我只是想来看看你。
Bù gànmá, wǒ zhǐ shì xiǎng lái kànkan nǐ.
儿子：我在做作业呢。
Wǒ zài zuò zuòyè ne.

Son: What for?
Mom: Nothing. Just want to have a look at you.
Son: I'm doing my homework.

G 4 哥哥。Gēge.

Elder brother

① 称呼同父母或只同父、只同母的兄长。
② 称呼同族或亲戚中的兄长。
③ 对年龄相近的男子的尊称。

Used to call one's elder brother or a male cousin who is older than oneself; Used as an honorific term to call any male older than oneself to show one's respect to the addressee.

G 5 给你。Gěi nǐ.

Here you are.

表示要把东西给予、交付给对方。

Used to mean one is giving something

to somebody.

简萍：给你。
Gěi nǐ.

甘玲：给我的生日礼物吗？谢谢！
Gěi wǒ de shēngrì lǐwù ma? Xièxiè!

简萍：祝你生日快乐！
Zhù nǐ shēngrì kuàilè!

Jian Ping: Here you are.
Gan Ling: A birthday present for me? Thank you so much.
Jian Ping: Happy birthday to you.

G 6 给我。Gěi wǒ.

Give it to me.

让对方把东西交付给自己。

Used to ask someone to give something to the speaker himself/herself.

林　海：给我。
Gěi wǒ.

丁小宁：凭什么给你？
Píng shénme gěi nǐ?

林　海：那原本就是我的东西啊。
Nà yuánběn jiùshì wǒ de dōngxī a.

丁小宁：给你就是了。
Gěi nǐ jiùshì le.

Lin Hai: Give it to me.
Ding Xiaoning: Why should I give it to you?
Lin Hai: Because it is mine.
Ding Xiaoning: Here you are.

G 7 贵姓。Guìxìng.

Your surname, please?

询问对方姓氏的敬语。

Used to inquire about one's family name.

小　刘：贵姓?
　　　　Guìxìng?
张先生：免贵姓张。
　　　　Miǎn guì xìng Zhāng.

Xiao Liu：Your surname, please?
Mr.Zhang：Zhang.

G 8 过来。Guòlai.

Come here.

让对方到自己这里来。

Used to ask someone to come up to the speaker himself/herself.

妈妈：过来。
Guòlai.
女儿：好的，来了，妈妈。
Hǎo de, lái le , māma.
Mum: Come here.
Daughter: Yes, Mum. I am coming.

H 1 好球！Hǎo qiú!

Bravo/Good shot/Good ball!.

赞叹球类运动中令人满意的击发与投射。

Used to hail a good performance in ball games.

林　海：好球！
Hǎoqiú!
丁小宁：好球！姚明又投了一个3分球。
Hǎo qiú! Yáo Míng yòu tóule yī gè 3 fēn qiú.
林　海：太棒了！
Tài bàng le!

Lin Hai: Bravo!.
Ding Xiaoning: Good ball! Yao Ming tapped another 3-point shot.
Lin Hai: Great!

H2 好热! Hǎo rè!

So hot!

表示温度很高。

Used to mean temperature is very high.

小韩：好热！
Hǎo rè!

小刘：今天最高气温有38℃。
Jīntiān zuì gāo qìwēn yǒu 38℃.

小韩：难怪，我的汗就一直没停过。
Nánguài, wǒ de hàn jiù yīzhí méi tíngguo.

Xiao Han: So hot!

Xiao Liu: The maximum temperature today is 38 ℃.

Xiao Han：No wonder I have been sweating all the day.

H3 好书! Hǎo shū!

A good book!

赞叹某本书。

Used to exclaim over a good book.

一个音节的句子 One-syllable Sentences

两个音节的句子 Two-syllable Sentences

三个音节的句子 Three-syllable Sentences

四个音节的句子 Four-syllable Sentences

林　海：好书！
Hǎo shū!
丁小宁：什么书让你这么着迷？
Shénme shū ràng nǐ zhème zháomí?
林　海：《三国演义》。
《Sān Guó Yǎnyì》.

Lin Hai: A good book!
Ding Xiaoning: What books are you so fascinated?
Lin Hai: "Romance of the Three Kingdoms".

H 4 和了。Hú le.

Hule

表示赢了，麻将游戏用语。

Used to mean one wins in a Mahjong game.

黄小姐：和了。
Hú le.
徐小姐：你又和了，你的手气太好了！
Nǐ yòu hú le, nǐ de shǒuqi tài hǎo le!
黄小姐：今天是挺顺的。
Jīntiān shì tǐngshùn de.

Ms. Huang: Hule.
Miss Xu: You have good lucks today!
Ms. Huang: Today is my lucky day.

H 5 坏了。Huài le.

It’s broken.

① 指出物品破损了。

Used to mean an item gets damaged.

简 萍：坏了。
Huài le.

丁小宁：摔坏了吗，手机？
Shuāi huàile ma, shǒujī?

简 萍：是啊，刚才不小心掉地上摔坏了。
Shì a, gāngcái bù xiǎoxīn diào dì shàng shuāihuài le.

Jian Ping: It’s broken
Ding Xiao Ning: Is your mobile phone broken?
Jian Ping: Yeah. It fell down the ground and got broken just now.

② 指出食物饮料等变质了。

Used to mean food or drink become decayed.

丈夫：坏了。
Huài le.
妻子：牛奶吗？坏了就不要喝了。
Niúnǎi ma? huài le jiù bùyào hē le.
Husband: Decayed.
Wife: Milk? Don' t drink the decayed milk.

③ 指出某些事情没有做好。

Used to mean one failed to do something well.

小刘：坏了。
Huài le.
小韩：怎么了？
Zěnme le?
小刘：煤气忘记关了，我得赶紧回家关上。
Méiqì wàngjì guān le, wǒ děi gǎnjǐn huíjiā guānshang.
小韩：你去吧。
Nǐ qù ba.
Xiao Liu: Dear me.
Xiao Han: What's wrong?
Xiao Liu: I forgot to turn off the gas. I have to hurry home to get it closed.
Xiao Han: Go back soon .

J 1 加油。Jiā yóu.

Come on/ Make an extra effort! /Jiayou!

① 鼓励对方加把劲儿。

Used to encourage a player to do better.

林　海：加油！
　　　　Jiāyóu!
丁小宁：谢谢。
　　　　Xièxiè.
林　海：你一定能赢。
　　　　Nǐ yīdìng néng yíng.

Lin Hai: Come on！ / Make an extra effort!
Ding Xiaoning: Thanks.
Lin Hai: You can surely win.

② 交通工具需要添加燃油。

Used to ask the gas station attendant to add fuel.

小　韩：加油。
　　　　Jiā yóu.
服务员：请问，加97号（汽油）吗?
　　　　Qǐngwèn, jiā 97 hào（qìyóu）ma?
小　韩：不是，加93号（汽油）.
　　　　Bùshi, jiā 93 hào（qìyóu）.

Xiao Han: Refuel.

Waiter: Excuse me, 97(gasoline) ?
Xiao Han: No, 93.

J 2 接着。Jiē zhe.

Catch/Hold it.

让对方把东西接住。

To ask someone to hold something that is being passed to him.

林　海：接着。
Jiē zhe.

丁小宁：好嘞，接住了，谢谢。
Hǎo lei , jiēzhù le, xièxie.

Lin Hai: Catch it.
Ding Xiaoning: Yes. Got it. Thanks.

J 3 姐夫。Jiěfu.

Brother-in-law

称呼姐姐的丈夫。

Used to call the husband of one's elder sister.

J 4 姐姐。Jiějie.

Sister

① 称呼同父母或只同父、只同母中年龄比自己大的女性。

② 称呼同辈亲戚中年龄比自己大的女性。

③ 称呼年轻的或年龄比自己略大的女性。

Used to call one's elder sister or a female cousin who is older than oneself; Used as an honorific term to call any female who is older than the speaker himself/herself to show one's respect to the addressee.

一个音节的句子 One-syllable Sentences
两个音节的句子 Two-syllable Sentences
三个音节的句子 Three-syllable Sentences
四个音节的句子 Four-syllable Sentences

J 5 借光。Jièguāng.

Excuse me

询问或请别人给予方便时说的套语。

Used to start an inquiry or to ask for help.

简萍：借光。（在教室，林海挡住简萍的路了。）
Jièguāng.（Zài jiàoshì, Lín Hǎi dǎngzhù le Jiǎn Píng de lù le.）

林海：啊?
Ā?

简萍：让我过去一下。
Ràng wǒ guòqù yī xià.

林海：不好意思。
Bù hǎo yìsi.

简萍：谢谢。
Xièxie.

Jian Ping: Excuse me. (In the classroom, Lin Hai is in Jian Ping's way)
Lin Hai: Ah?
Jian Ping: Excuse me, You are in my way.
Woodlands: Sorry.
Jian Ping: That's all right. Thank you.

K 1 开始。Kāishǐ.

Let's begin/start/go.

可以着手进行某项工作或活动了。

Used to ask someone to start to do something.

老师：开始。
（考场上，学生们听到老师的指令后开始做答卷。）
Kāishǐ.
(Kǎochǎng shàng, xuéshēngmen tīngdao lǎoshī de zhǐlìng hòu kāishǐ zuò dájuàn.)

Teacher: Examination starts.
(In the examination classroom, the students began to have an exam upon hearing the teacher's instructions.)

K 2 快点儿。kuàidiǎnr.

Hurry up!

催促对方加快速度。

Used to urge someone to make hurry.

妻子：快点儿！
Kuàidiǎnr?
丈夫：别催我了！
Bié cuī wǒ le?
妻子：不然，就赶不上车了。
Bùrán, jiù gǎnbushàng chē le.

Wife: Hurry up!
Husband: Do not rush me!
Wife: Otherwise we will miss the bus.

K 3 快来。Kuài lái.

Come quickly.

催促对方快点儿过来。

Used to urge someone to come quickly.

林　海：快来。
Kuài lái.
丁小宁：来了。
Lái le.
林　海：快点儿，比赛马上开始了。
Kuàidiǎnr, bǐsài mǎshang kāishǐ le.

Lin Hai: Come quickly.
Ding Xiaoning: I am coming.
Lin Hai: Hurry up. The contest will start soon.

L 1 劳驾。Láojià.

Excuse me.

请别人做事或让路时的客套话。

Used as a polite way to ask for help or to make a way for the speaker himself /herself.

小韩：劳驾。
Láojià.
小刘：什么事?
Shénme shì?
小韩：请让一下。
Qǐng ràng yīxià.

Xiao Han: Excuse me.
Xiao Liu: What's the matter?
Xiao Han: Please make way for me.

L 2 老弟。Lǎodì.

Brother.

① 呼喊弟弟。
② 称呼比自己年纪小的男性。

Used to call one's younger brother or a male friend who is younger than oneself.

L 3 姥姥。LǎoLao.

Grandma.

称呼母亲的母亲。

Used to call one's mother's mother.

L 4 老师。Lǎoshī.

Teacher.

对教师的尊称。

Used as an honorific term to call teachers.

L 5 老兄。Lǎoxiōng.

Big brother.

① 称呼兄长。
Used as an honorific term to call one's elder brother.

② 男性朋友相互之间的敬称。
Used as an honorific term to call one's male friends.

L 5 姥爷。Lǎoye.

Grandpa.

称呼母亲的父亲。
Used to call one's mother's father.

L 6 累吗？ Lèi ma?

Are you tired?

询问对方是否疲乏、劳累。

Used to ask if someone is tired.

妻子：累吗？
Lèi ma?

丈夫：中午都没休息，有点儿累啦。
Zhōngwǔ dōu méi xiūxī, yǒudiǎnr lèi la.

Wife: Are you tired?
Husband: I haven't had a nap, so I feel a little bit tired now.

L 7 靓女。Liàngnǚ.

Beauty/Miss/Waitress.

呼喊年轻的女子，一般在广东、香港地区使用。

Used in Guangdong and Hong Kong to call girls or young ladies.

徐小姐：靓女。
Liàngnǚ.
服务员：有什么事可以帮您?
Yǒu shénme shì kěyǐ bāng nín?
徐小姐：请泡壶茶。
Qǐng pào hú chá.
服务员：您稍等。
Nín shāoděng.

Miss Xu: Waitress.
Waitress: What can I do to help?
Miss Xu: Please make a pot of tea for us.
Waiter: Just a moment.

L 8 靓仔。Liàngzǎi.

Smart boy/Waiter.

称呼年轻的男子，一般在广东、香港地区使用。

Used in Guangdong and Hong Kong to call boys or young men.

顾　客：靓仔。
Liàngzǎi.
服务员：您好，有什么事可以帮您?
Nínhǎo, yǒu shénme shì kěyǐ bāng nín?
顾　客：刚才忘了说，牛排要五成熟的。
Gāngcái wàng le shuō, niúpái yào wǔ chéng shú de.

服务员：好的。
Hǎo de.

Miss Xu: Waiter.
Waiter: Yes? Is there anything I can do for you?
Miss Xu: Just forget to tell you. I want the steak half stewed.
Waiter: Ok.

M 1 妈妈。Māma.

Mum.

称呼母亲。

Used to call one's mother.

M 2 慢点儿。Màndiǎnr.

Slowly, slowly.

让对方降低速度，不要太快。

Used to ask someone to slow down.

妈妈：慢点儿。（妈妈看见儿子吃饭太快。）
Màndiǎnr.（Māma kànjiàn érzi chīfàn tàikuài.）

儿子：我太饿了，妈妈。
Wǒ tài è le, māma.
妈妈：吃太快会噎到的。
Chī tài kuài huì yēdao de.

Mom: slowly. (The mother saw her son eat too fast.)
Son: I was too hungry, Mom.
Mom: You will get choked if you eat too fast.

M 3 忙吗？ Máng ma？

Are you busy?

询问事情是否多。

Used to ask if someone is busy at the moment or recently.

小韩：忙吗?
Máng ma?
小刘：还行，不太忙，有事儿吗?
Háixíng , bù tài máng, yǒushìr ma?
小韩：有个问题想请教你。
Yǒu gè wèntí xiǎng qǐngjiào nǐ.
小刘：别客气，你说。
Bié kèqi, nǐ shuō.

Xiao Han: Are you busy now?
Xiao Liu: Not too busy. what's the matter?
Xiao Han: I have a question to ask you.
Xiao Liu: Just tell me what it is.

M 4 妹妹。Mèimei.

Sister.

① 称呼同父母或只同父、只同母中年龄比自己小的女性。

② 称呼同辈中年龄比自己小的女性。

Used to call one's younger sister or a female cousin who is younger than oneself; Used to call a female who is younger than oneself.

M 5 明儿见。Míngr jiàn.

See you tomorrow.

与人道别时的话，表示明天再见。

Used to say goodbye between two people who will see each other the next day.

N 1 奶奶。Nǎinai.

Grandma.

① 呼喊父亲的母亲。

② 称呼祖母辈中的女性。

Used to call one's father's mother or an elderly lay who is of one's grandmother's age.

N 2 你好！Nǐ hǎo!

How do you do!

问候语。

Used to greet someone in a formal way.

N 3 你是……？ Nǐ shì……？

You are…?

询问对方的身份。

Used to inquire about the name of somebody

小　刘：你是……？
　　　　Nǐ shì ……？
林先生：我是新来的，姓林，你好。
　　　　Wǒ shì xīn lái de, xìng Lín, nǐ hǎo.

Xiao Liu: You are…?
Mr Lin: I am a new comer. My family name is Liu. How do you do!

N 4 你早。Nǐ zǎo.

Morning!

早上见面时的问候语，同“早安”。

Used to greet each other in the morning.

N 5 您好！ Nín hǎo!

How do you do!

问候语，是“你好”的敬称。

Used as an honorific term for greeting.

N 6 您早！ Nín zǎo!

Good morning!

早上见面时的问候语。

Used as an honorific way to greet each other in the morning.

P 1 怕啥？ Pà shá?

What are you in fear of?

询问对方害怕什么。

Used to inquire what one is in fear of.

哥哥：怕啥?
Pà shá?
弟弟：那里有条蛇。
Nàli yǒu tiáo shé.

Elder Brother: What are you in fear of?
Younger Brother: There is a snake over there.

P 2 婆婆。Pó po.

Mother-in-Law.

① 称呼父亲的母亲。
② 称呼丈夫的母亲。
③ 称呼祖母辈中的女性。

Used to call one's father's mother;
Used to call one's husband's mother;
Used to call any elderly ladies of grandma's age.

Q 1 沏茶。Qī chá.

Make a cup of tea, please.

让对方泡茶。

Used to ask someone(usually waiter) to make a cup of tea.

徐小姐：请沏茶。
Qǐng qīchá.
服务员：好的，您稍等。
Hǎo de, nín shāoděng.

Miss Xu: A cup of tea, please.
Waiter: Yes. Just a moment.

Q 2 请进。Qǐngjìn.

Come in, please.

请对方进来。
Used to ask someone to come into a room.

Q 3 请坐。Qǐngzuò.

Sit down, please.

请对方坐下。
Used to ask someone to take a seat.

Q 4 取钱。Qǔqián.

I want to withdraw some money.

告诉银行业务员自己要把钱取出来。

To ask the clerk to withdraw some money from the bank account.

小　刘：取钱。
Qǔqián.

业务员：请问取多少?
Qǐngwèn qǔ duōshao?

小　刘：把卡里的钱全部取出来。
Bǎ kǎ li de qián quánbù qǔ chūlái.

业务员：您稍等。
Nín shāoděng.

Xiao Liu: I want to withdraw some money.
Clerk: How much, please?
Xiao Liu: I want to withdraw all the money in this card.
Clerk: Please wait a moment.

S 1 嫂子。Sǎozi.

Sister-in-law

① 称呼兄长的妻子。
② 朋友妻子的敬呼。

Used to call one's elder brother's wife; A general term used to call married women.

S 2 上课。Shàngkè.

Let's begin our class./Class begins.

提示一节课就要开始了。

Used to tell students to start having a class.

老　师：上课。
Shàngkè.

班　长：起立。
Qǐlì.

同学们：老师好。
Lǎoshī hǎo.

老　师：同学们好，坐下。
Tóngxuémen hǎo, zuòxia.

Teacher: Let's begin our class.
Monitor: Stand up.
Students: Good morning/afternoon, teacher.
Teacher: Sit down, please.

S 3 谁的？ Shéi de?

Whose is it?

询问某样东西属于谁。
Used to ask whom something belongs to.

小韩：谁的?
　　Shuí de?
小刘：杯子吗？ 哦，我的。
　　Bēizi ma? ò, wǒ de.

Xiao Han: Whose cup is it?
Xiao Liu: This cup? Oh, it's mine.

S 4 谁呀？ Shéi ya?

Who is it?

同"谁？"
To have the same meaning as "谁?"

S 5 婶婶。Shěnshen.

Aunty

称呼叔叔的妻子。
Used to call uncle's wife.

S 6 叔叔。Shūshu.

Uncle.

① 称呼父亲的弟弟。
② 泛称与父亲同辈而年龄较小的男性。

Used to call one's father's younger brother; Used to call the male who are of the same generation but younger than one's father.

T 1 躺下。Tǎngxia.

Lie down, please.

让对方将身体横倒。
Used to ask someone to lie down.

医生：躺下。
Tǎngxià.
病人：（病人躺下。）医生，是平躺着吗?
(bìngrén tǎngxia.) Yīshēng, shì píng tǎng zhe ma?
医生：是的。哪里痛?
Shì de. nǎli tòng?
病人：肚子疼。
Dùzi téng.

Doctor: Lie down.
Patient: (The patient lies down.) Doctor, need I lie flat?
Doctor: Yes. Where do you feel pain?
Patient: stomach.

T 2 疼吗? Téng ma?

Do you feel pain ?

询问对方是否有疼痛的感觉。
Used to ask if someone feels pain.

护士：疼吗?
Téng ma?
孩子：不疼。
Bùténg.
护士：真勇敢。
Zhēn yǒnggǎn.

Nurse: Do you feel pain?
Children: No pain.
Nurse: A brave boy.

T 3 天哪！ Tiān na!

Unbelievable/My Goodness!

因极度惊讶而发出的惊叹，表示不可思议和不敢相信。

Used to exclaim over something that happened because it seemed incredible or unbelievable.

妻子：天哪！
Tiān na!
丈夫：什么事儿?
Shénme shìr?
妻子：我中奖了，一百万。
Wǒ zhōng jiǎng le, yī bǎi wàn.
Wife: My Goodness!
Husband: What's the matter?
Wife: I hit the jackpot, one million.

一个音节的句子
One-syllable Sentences
两个音节的句子
Two-syllable Sentences
三个音节的句子
Three-syllable Sentences
四个音节的句子
Four-syllable Sentences

T 4 停车。Tíngchē.

Stop.

请对方把车停下来。

Used to ask someone to stop the car.

交警：停车。
Tíngchē.
司机：怎么了？
Zěnme le?
交警：查车。
Chá chē.

Police: Stop!.
Drivers: What's wrong, sir?
Police: Traffic check.

T 5 退票。Tuìpiào.

Please refund my ticket for me.

把买好的票（车票、船票或电影票等）退还给售票处，并收回相应的买票钱。

Used when returning tickets (train tickets, bus tickets, ferry tickets or movie tickets, etc.) to the ticket office for getting back the money.

买票者：退票。
Tuìpiào.

售票员：退票要扣20%的手续费。
Tuìpiào yào kòu 20% de shǒuxùfèi.

买票者：没问题。
Méi wèn tí.

Buy tickets: Please refund my ticket for me.
Conductor: 20% refunding charge.
Buy a ticket: No problem.

W 1 外公。Wàigōng.

Grandpa.

称呼母亲的父亲。
Used to call one's mother's father.

一个音节的句子 One-syllable Sentences
两个音节的句子 Two-syllable Sentences
三个音节的句子 Three-syllable Sentences
四个音节的句子 Four-syllable Sentences

W 2 外婆。Wàipó.

Grandma.

称呼母亲的母亲。
Used to call one's mother's mother.

W 3 晚安。Wǎn'ān.

Good night!

晚上，发话者向对方表示问候或道别的客套话。
Used to say good bye when departing in the night.

X 1 先生。Xiānsheng.

Sir/Gentleman.

称呼成年男性。
Used as an honorific term to call a male adult.

X 2 咸了。Xián le.

Too salty

认为味道太咸。

Used to mean food is too salty.

丈夫：咸了。
Xián le.

妻子：糟糕，刚才可能放了两次盐。
Zāogāo, gāngcái kěnéng fàngle liǎng cì yán.

Husband: Eww! Too salty.

Wife: Jesus (Christ)! I must have put salt twice.

X 3 小姐。Xiǎojei.

Miss.

称呼年轻的女子。

Used to call young ladies.

X 4 小偷。Xiǎotōu.

Thief!

本义是指偷东西的人，话语中通常是提醒有小偷。

Used to remind people that there is a thief or there are some thieves nearby.

小韩：小偷。
Xiǎotōu.
乘客：抓住他。
Zhuāzhù tā.

Xiao Han: He is a thief.
Passengers: Catch him.

X 5 小心。Xiǎoxīn.

Be cautious /Be careful.

提醒对方要谨慎、留神。同“当心”。

Used to advise someone to be cautious.

X 6 小姨。Xiǎoyí.

Aunty.

称呼母亲最小的妹妹。
Used to call one's mother's youngest sister.

Y 1 姨夫。Yífu.

Uncle.

称呼母亲的姐姐或妹妹的丈夫。
Used to call the husband of one's mother's sister.

Y 2 姨妈。Yímā.

Aunt.

称呼母亲已经结婚的姐妹。
Used to call a married sister of one's mother.

一个音节的句子 One-syllable Sentences
两个音节的句子 Two-syllable Sentences
三个音节的句子 Three-syllable Sentences
四个音节的句子 Four-syllable Sentences

Y 3 爷爷。Yéye.

Grandpa.

① 称呼父亲的父亲。
② 对男性老人的尊称。
Used to call one's father's father;
Used as an honorific term to call an elderly man of grandpa's age.

Z 1 糟糕。Zāogāo.

Oops/Dear me/
Jesus(Christ)/ Oh!.

表示事情出现坏情况。
Used to show something bad will happen or has happened.

黄小姐：糟糕！
Zāogāo!
徐小姐：怎么了？
Zěnme le!
黄小姐：要下雨了，衣服还晾在外面呢。
Yào xiàyǔ le, yīfu hái liàng zài wàimiàn ne.

Ms. Huang: Oops!
Miss Xu: What's wrong?
Ms. Huang: It's going to rain, but I forget to pick up the clothes. They are put in the open air.

Z 2 再见! Zàijiàn!

Good-bye!

希望以后能够再见面，道别时的客套话。
Used to express one's wish to see someone again when departing.

Z 3 啧啧。Zézé.

Oh, my/Gee!

表示赞扬、叹息、惊异等。
Used to express one's admiration

or surprise.

小韩：啧啧。
Zé zé.
小刘：怎么了？
Zěnme le?
小韩：你看这画儿上的马，就像要狂奔出来似的。
Nǐ kàn zhè huàr shàng de mǎ, jiù xiàng yào kuángbēn chūlai shìde.

Xiao Han: Oh, my /Gee.
Xiao Liu: What's up?
Xiao Han: Look at the horse on the painting, it's painted so lively that it seems it is going to run out of the painting.

Z 4 真黑！ Zhēn hēi!

How dark/black.

① 感叹颜色很黑。

Used to mean something is as black as coal.

黄小姐：真黑。
Zhēn hēi.
徐小姐：什么？
Shénme?
黄小姐：你的头发。
Nǐ de tóufa.

Miss. Huang: How black it is.
Miss Xu: What?
Miss. Huang: Your hair.

② 表示光线不足。

Used to mean there is no(enough) light in a room.

妈妈：真黑。
Zhēnhēi.
儿子：是啊，屋子里光线不太好。不过没关系，开灯就行了。
Shì a, wūzi li guāngxiàn bù tài hǎo. bùguò méi guānxi, kāidēng jiù xíng le.
Mom: So dark.
Son: Yeah. There isn't enough light in the room. It doesn't matter. We can turn on the lights.

③ 谴责那些采取各种手段损害其他人利益的行为。

Used to critise some people who are bad or wicked.

小韩：真黑！
Zhēn hēi!
小刘：真是太黑了。过了期的牛奶还拿出来卖。
Zhēnshì tài hēi le. guòle qī de niúnǎi hái ná chūlai mài.

小韩：他们只想着赚钱，根本不顾别人的死活。
Tāmen zhǐ xiǎngzhe zhuànqián, gēnběn bùgù biérén de sǐhuó.

Xiao Han: How wicked.
Xiao Liu: Yes, too wicked. How can they sell the expired milk?
Xiao Han: They just want to make money without considering the health of others.

Z 5 真快。Zhēn kuài.

How fast it is!/ How time flies!

① 表示速度很快。

Used to mean the speed is very fast.

小韩：真快。
Zhēn kuài.
小刘：当然啦，高铁的时速可以达到每小时350多公里呢。
Dāngrán la, gāotiě de shísù kěyǐ dádào měi xiǎoshí 350 duō gōnglǐ ne.

Xiao Han: How fast it is!
Xiao Liu: Of course, the speed of high-speed rail can be as fast as over 350 kilometers per hour.

② 表示时间过得快。

Used to mean time flies.

小韩：真快。
Zhēn kuài.

小刘：是啊，五天这么快就过去了。
Shì a, wǔ tiān zhème kuài jiù guòqu le.

小韩：我真不想走，这地方太美了。明年，我还来。
Wǒ zhēn bù xiǎng zǒu, zhè dìfang tài měi le. míngnián, wǒ hái lái.

Xiao Han: How time files.
Xiao Liu: Yeah. Five days have passed so quickly.
Xiao Han: This place is so beautiful that I am reluctant to leave. This time next year, I will come back again.

Z 6 真累！ Zhēn lèi!

Exhausted!

表示疲乏，一般指身体上的或心理上的。

Used to mean one is physically or psychologically fatigue.

丈夫：真累！
Zhēn lèi!

妻子：你最近一直加班，当然累啦。
Nǐ zuìjìn yīzhí jiābān, dāngrán lèi la.

Husband: Exhausted!

Wife: You have been working overtime recently. Surely you will feel tired.

Z 7 真慢！ Zhēn màn!

How slow it is!

表示速度慢。

To mean the speed is very slow.

简萍：真慢！
Zhēn màn!
甘玲：没办法，堵车嘛。
Méi bànfa, dǔchē ma.

Jian Ping: Really slow.
Gan Ling: It can't be helped. A traffic jam in rush hour.

Z 8 真甜！ Zhēn tián!

sweet!

表示味道甜。

Used to mean something(usually a fruit)is very sweet.

女儿：真甜！
Zhēn tián!
妈妈：这是新疆的哈密瓜，当然甜了。
Zhè shì Xīnjiāng de hāmìguā, dāngrán tián le.

Daughter: It tastes really sweet.
Mom: Of course it is sweet. It is Xinjiang Hami melon.

Z 9 真鲜！Zhēn xiān!

Very tasty /delicious.

表示味道鲜美。

Used to mean some food(or soup) is very delicious.

丈夫：真鲜！
Zhēn xiān!

妻子：我放了新鲜的松茸进去，汤就更鲜了。
Wǒ fàngle xīnxiān de sōngróng jìnqu, tāng jiù gèng xiān le.

丈夫：怪不得。
Guàibude.

Husband: Really delicious.

Wife: I put some fresh matsutake into the soup to add some flavor.

Husband: No wonder it tastes so delicious.

Z10 真咸！ Zhēn xián!

Very salty!

表示味道太咸了。

Used to mean something(usually a food) is very salty.

丈夫：真咸!
Zhēn xián!

妻子：盐放多了
Yán fàng duō le.

Husband: Taste very/too salty.
Wife: There is too much salt in them.

Z11 真香！ Zhēn xiāng!

Very tasty /delicious/fragrant.

① 表示味道好。

Used to mean some food is very delicious.

女儿：真香！
Zhēn xiāng!
妈妈：那就多吃点儿。
Nà jiù duō chī diǎnr.
女儿：谢谢妈妈。
Xièxie māma.
Daughter: Very tasty /delicious!
Mom: Then help yourself & have more.
Daughter: Thank you, Mom.

② 表示气味好闻。

Used to mean something smells good/fragrant.

黄小姐：真香。
Zhēn xiāng.
徐小姐：好闻吗?
Hǎo wén ma?
黄小姐：很好闻。什么牌子的?
Hěn hǎo wén. shénme páizi de?
徐小姐：香奈儿，这一季新出的一款香水。
Xiāngnǎi'r, zhè yī jì xīn chū de yī kuǎn xiāngshuǐ.
Miss. Huang: Very fragrant..
Miss Xu: Does it smell good?
Miss. Huang: Yeah, very good smell. What brand?
Miss Xu: Chanel. Newly produced perfume.

Z12 真悬!
Zhēn xuán!

What a narrow escape!

觉得惊险时的感叹。

Used to exclaim over one's narrow escape from a danger.

小韩：真悬!

Zhēn xuán!

小刘：就是，要不是早上岸了，一定会被浪卷走的。

Jiùshì, yàobushì zǎo shàng àn le, yīdìng huì bèi làng juǎnzǒu de.

小韩：是啊。

Shì a.

Xiao Han: What a narrow escape!

Xiao Liu: If we hadn't come up to the bank timely, we would have been swept away by the waves.

Xiao Han: You said it.

A 1 哎呦，疼。
Āiyōu, téng.

Ouch. It hurts.

叫唤一声，表示疼痛。

Used as show one feels pain.

病人：哎呦，疼。
Āiyōu, téng.

医生：忍一下，给伤口消毒会有些疼的，一会儿就好了。
Rěn yíxià, gěi shāngkǒu xiāodú huì yǒuxiē téng de, yīhuìr jiù hǎo le.

Patient: Ouch. It hurts.

Doctor: Hold on. To disinfect wounds will cause some pain.it will be done right now.

A 2 挨打了？
Ái dǎ le?

Got beaten?

询问对方是否被人打了，表示关心。

Used to ask whether someone was beaten so as to show one's concern.

丁小宁：挨打了？
Āi dǎ le?
林　海：没有啊。
Méiyǒu a.
丁小宁：怎么额头上青一块。
Zěnme étóu shang qīngle yī kuài.
林　海：哦，不小心碰的。
Ò, bù xiǎoxīn pèng de.

Ding Xiaoning: Got beaten?
Lin Hai: No.
Ding Xiaoning: Why do you have a blue in your forehead.
Lin Hai: Oh, I carelessly get it knocked somewhere.

B 1 包丢了。Bāo diū le.

My bag gets lost.

告诉对方自己的钱包、提包之类的物品丢失了。
Used to tell someone that one's bag gets lost.

黄小姐：包丢了。
Bāo diū le.
徐小姐：你是不是放在吃饭的地方忘记拿了？
Nǐ shìbushì fàng zài chīfàn de dìfang wàngjì ná le?

黄小姐：我想想，是啊，是落在吃饭的地方了。
Wǒ xiǎngxiang, shì a , shì là zài chīfàn de dìfang le.

徐小姐：赶快去找。
Gǎnkuài qù zhǎo.

Miss. Huang: My bag gets lost.
Miss Xu: Didn't you leave it behind in the place you had your meal?
Miss. Huang: Let me think. Yes, I left it there.
Miss Xu: Let's go to fetch it now.

B 2 别吵了。 Bié chǎo le.

Be quiet/Stop/quarreling!

① 要求对方安静，不要吵闹。
Used to ask others to be quiet.

② 制止吵架。
Used to stop a quarrel.

（自习课上，有两个同学正在吵架。）
（zìxí kè shàng, yǒu liǎng gè tóngxué zhèngzài chǎojià.）

班长：别吵了！
Bié chǎo le !

林海：你们就别吵了，大家还要做作业呢。
Nǐmén jiù bié chǎo le, dàjiā háiyào zuò zuòyè ne.

(Two students are quarreling in a self-study class)

Monitor: Stop quarreling!

Lin Hai: Don't quarrel anymore. We are doing homework.

B 3 别闹了。
Bié nǎo le.

Quiet, please/Stop making laughter.

要求不要吵嚷。

Used to ask others to be quiet or stop making laughters.

班长：别闹了！
Bié nào le!

丁小宁：好了，不闹了，该干正事了。
Hǎo le, bù nào le, gāi gàn zhèngshì le.

Monitor: Be quiet, please!

Ding Xiaoning: Stop making laughter, boys & girls. Let's settle down to our business.

一个音节的句子 One-syllable Sentences
两个音节的句子 Two-syllable Sentences
三个音节的句子 Three-syllable Sentences
四个音节的句子 Four-syllable Sentences

B 4 别呛着。
Bié qiāngzhe.

Do not choke yourself!

提醒喝水或吃饭的人慢点儿，以免水或食物进入气管引起不适或危险。

Used to remind someone to drink or eat slowly in case water or food enters into the trachea to cause discomfort or danger.

（儿子端起杯子就大口大口地喝水。）
（Érzi duānqi bēizi jiù dà kǒu dà kǒu de hē shuǐ.）

妈妈：别呛着。
Bié qiang zhe.

儿子：嗯。
Ǹ.

妈妈：慢点儿喝。
Màn diǎnr hē.

(The son was gulping down a glass of water.)
Mom: Do not choke yourself.
Son: Um.
Mom: Drink slowly.

B 5 别生气。Bié shēngqì.

Don’t be angry.

劝说对方不要生气。

Used to persuade someone not to get angry.

黄小姐：别生气。
Bié shēngqì.

徐小姐：我能不生气吗？你看他把我说成什么样儿了！
Wǒ néng bù shēngqì ma? nǐ kàn tā bǎ wǒ shuō chéng shénme yàngr le!

Miss Huang: Do not be angry.

Miss Xu: Can’t I get angry? You know how he abased/ belittled me !

B 6 别噎着。
Bié yēzhe.

Don't choke yourself .

提醒和劝告对方吃东西不要太快，以免食物塞住食道难以下咽。

Used to warn someone not to eat too fast in case the food will stuff the throat to cause discomfort or danger.

妈妈：别噎着。
Bié yēzhe.

儿子：没办法，得快点儿吃，赶时间呢。
Méi bànfǎ, děi kuàidiǎnr chī, gǎn shíjiān ne.

妈妈：噎着就难受了。
Yēzhe jiù nánshòu le.

Mom: Don't choke yourself.
Son: I have to eat fast. I am in a great hurry.
Mom: If you choke yourself, you'll suffer a lot.

B 7 病了吗? Bìngle ma?

Are you ill?

询问是否生病了，表示关心。

Used to ask somebody if he or she is ill or not so as to show the speaker's concern on him.

小韩：病了吗?
　　　Bìngle ma?
小刘：是啊，感冒了。
　　　Shì a, gǎnmào le.
小韩：要不要休息?
　　　Yào buyào xiūxi?
小刘：不用了，问题不大。
　　　Bùyòng le, wèntí bù dà.

Xiao Han: Are you ill?
Xiao Liu: Yes, I caught a cold yesterday.
Xiao Han: Do you a need a half-day rest?
Xiao Liu: No, it's not serious. I can make it through.

C 1 车坏了。
Chē huài le.

The car has broken/down.

车出问题了，不能继续行驶。

Used to show something is wrong with the car so that it doesn't work.

小韩：车坏了。
Chē huài le.

小刘：糟糕，我还急着去开会呢。
Zāogāo, wǒ hái jízhe qù kāihuì ne.

小韩：要不，你坐出租先走？
Yàobù, nǐ zuò chūzū xiān zǒu?

小刘：只有这样了。不好意思，我先走了。
Zhǐyǒu zhèyàng le. bùhǎoyìsi, wǒ xiān zǒu le.

小韩：没关系。
Méi guānxi.

Xiao Han: The car has broken down.
Xiao Liu: Oh my god, I have a meeting to attend.
Xiao Han: What about you take a taxi and go first?
Xiao Liu: This is just what I can do now. Sorry that I have to go first.
Xiao Han: It doesn't matter.

C 2 车来了。Chē lái le.

Here comes the bus.

① 告诉对方车来了。

Used to tell somebody the bus is coming.

黄小姐：车来了。
Chē lái le.

徐小姐：那我就准备上车了。
Nà wǒ juì zhǔnbèi shàngchē le.

Miss Huang: Here comes the bus.
Miss Xu: Well，I am getting on the bus.

② 表示有车出现，有提醒注意安全的意思。

Used to remind somebody to be careful when any vehicle is approaching.

王小姐：车来了。
Chē lái le.

徐小姐：啊?
Ā?

（王小姐拉着徐小姐避开汽车。）
（Wáng Xiǎojie lāzhe Xú Xiǎojie bìkāi qìchē.）

徐小姐：真险！
Zhēn xiǎn！

Miss Wang: Here comes a bus.
Miss Xu: What?
(Miss Wang was pulling Miss Xu to avoid the bus.)
Miss Xu: What a narrow escape!

C 3 吃饭没？ Chīfàn méi?

Have you had your breakfast/lunch/supper?

见面时（一般在吃饭前后的这段时间）打招呼。

Used as a way of greeting (usually at the usual time of having a meal).

（上午刚上班，小韩遇见小刘。）
（Shàngwǔ gāng shàngbān, Xiǎo Hán yùjiàn Xiǎo Liú.）

小韩：吃饭没？
Chīfàn méi?

小刘：吃过了。你呢？
Chīguò le. nǐ ne?

小韩：我也吃过了。
Wǒ yě chīguò le.

(Xiao Han met Xiao Liu in the office when he just started to work in the morning)
Xiao Han: Have you had your breakfast?
Xiao Liu: Yes, what about you?
Xiao Han: Me too.

C 4 出发吧。
Chū fā ba.

Let's go.

建议或宣布启程。
Used to suggest starting a journey.

D 1 打扰了。
Dǎrǎo le.

Excuse me.

接受招待或请求别人帮助时表示歉意的客套话。

一个音节的句子 One-syllable Sentences
两个音节的句子 Two-syllable Sentences
三个音节的句子 Three-syllable Sentences
四个音节的句子 Four-syllable Sentences

Used to show one's politeness when one is served or helped by others.

小韩：打扰了。
Dǎrǎo le.

小刘：有事吗?
Yǒu shì ma?

小韩：想请你帮忙查个资料。
Xiǎng qǐng nǐ bāngmáng chá gè zīliào.

小刘：没问题。
méi wèntí.

Xiaohan: Excuse me.
Xiaoliu: Can I help you?
Xiaohan: Yes. Can you help me to search for some information?
Xiaoliu: Sure, no problem.

D 2 等等我。
Děngdeng wǒ.

Wait for me.

请求别人等候自己。同“等等。”
Used to ask someone to wait for the speaker himself / herself, meaning “Wait for a minute”.

D 3 等一下。Děng yīxià.

Wait a minute.

希望别人等候一会儿。

Used to ask someone to wait a moment.

收银员：等一下。
Děng yīxià.

甘　玲：为什么？
Wèishénme?

收银员：我还没找您钱呢。
Wǒ hái méi zhǎo nín qián ne.

Cashier: Wait a minute.
Gan Ling: What for?
Cashier: Your changes，please.

D 4 对不起。Duìbuqǐ.

Sorry.

表达歉意的礼貌用语。

Used to show one's apology.

D 5 多少钱? Duōshao qián?

How much?

询问商品的价格。

Used to ask the price .

甘　玲：多少钱?
Duōshao qián?
售货员：五块钱一斤。
Wǔ kuài qián yī jīn.
甘　玲：我要两斤。
Wǒ yào liǎng jīn.

Gan Ling: How much?
Salesman: Five Yuan.
Gan Ling: I would like 1Kg.

F 1 发烧吗? Fāshāo ma?

Do you have a fever?

询问体温是否过高。

Used to ask whether somebody is running a feuer.

医生：发烧吗？
Fāshāo ma?
病人：刚刚护士量过，37.1℃。
Gānggāng hùshì liáng guò, 37.1℃.
医生：有点儿烧。
Yǒudiǎnr shāo.

Doctor: Do you have a fever?
Patient: The nurse has just taken it, it's 37.1℃.
Doctor: You have got a fever.

F 2 房卡呢？ Fángkǎ ne?

Where is the room card?

询问房卡在哪里。
Used to ask where the room card is.

小 刘：房卡呢？
Fángkǎ ne?
服务员：您稍等，我这就给您。
Nín shāoděng, wǒ zhè jiù gěi nín.
小 刘：谢谢。
Xièxie.

Xiao Liu: Where is the room card?
Atlendant: Sorry, I forgot it. Please wait a minute. Here you are.
Xiao Liu: Thank you.

F 3

服务员。
Fúwùyuán.

Waiter/Waitress.

呼叫宾馆、酒店等服务行业中直接为顾客服务的人员

Used to call the people who provide services in hotel or restaurant, etc.

G 1

干吗呢？
Gànmá ne?

What are you doing?

询问对方在做什么事情。

Used to ask what the listener is doing at this moment.

甘玲：干吗呢？
Gànmá ne?

简萍：在给我妈妈写邮件。
Zài gěi wǒ māma xiě yóujiàn.

Gan Ling: What are you doing?

Jian Ping: I am writing an e-mail to my mother.

G 2 给，换上。Gěi, huànshàng.

Here it is. Put it on.

给对方东西以替换原来的东西（如衣服）。

Used to give somebody something (e.g. a clothes or a pair of shoes) in order to replace the old ones.

妈妈：给，换上。
Gěi, huànshàng.

女儿：好漂亮的鞋啊！谢谢妈妈！
Hǎo piàoliang de xié a！xièxie māma！

Mum: Here are the new pair of shoes. Put them on.

Daughter: What a pretty pair of shoes. Thank you, mum!

一个音节的句子 One-syllable Sentences
两个音节的句子 Two-syllable Sentences
三个音节的句子 Three-syllable Sentences
四个音节的句子 Four-syllable Sentences

G 3 给你吧。
Gěi nǐ ba.

Here you are.

给对方东西。

Used to mean one wants to give somebody something.

黄小姐：给你吧。
Gěi nǐ bā.
徐小姐：好的，谢谢！
Hǎo de, xièxie !

Miss Huang: Here you are.
Miss Xu: Thank you!

G 4 给您钱。
Gěi nín qián.

Here's the money.

将钱给对方。

Used to mean one wants to give some money to somebody.

甘玲：给您钱。
Gěi nín qián.
收银员：好的。这是找您的钱，请收好。
Hǎode, zhè shì zhǎo nín de qián, qǐng shōuhǎo.
Gan Ling: Here's the money.
Cashier: Thanks. Here is the change. Please keep it.

H 1 还行吗？ Hái xíng ma?

Is that ok/Can you/carry it?

① 询问对方是否满意。

Used to ask whether someone is satisfied with something.

甘玲：还行吗？
Hái xíng ma?
简萍：写得很好，尤其是对人物心理的描写。
Xiě de hěn hǎo, yóuqí shì duì rénwù xīnlǐ de miáoxiě.
甘玲：谢谢。
Xièxie.

Gan Ling: Is that ok?
Jian Ping: It's wonderful, especially the psychological description of the characters.
Gan Ling: Thank you.

② 询问对方是否还有能力做某事。

Used to ask whether someone can do something.

小刘：还行吗？
Hái xíng ma?
小韩：没问题。搬这点儿东西，不算什么。
Méi wèntí. bān zhèdiǎnr dōngxi, bùsuàn shénme.

Xiao Liu: Can you carry it?
Xiao Han: No problem, it's not a big deal to carry these things.

H 2 好吵啊！ Hǎo chǎo a!

How noisy it is!

抱怨环境杂乱、吵闹。

Used to complain that a place is noisy and out of order.

小刘：好吵啊。
Hǎo chǎo a.
小韩：下面就是菜市场，到晚上才会安静会儿。
Xiàmiàn jiùshì cài shìchǎng, dào wǎnshàng cái huì ānjìng huìr.

Xiao Liu: How noisy it is!
Xiao Han: Yes, there is a free market downstairs; it can be quiet only in the evening.

H 3 好吃吧? Hǎochī ba!

Yummy, huh?

自己认为某种食物好吃，请对方品尝，并同意自己的看法。

Used to ask somebody to taste something which one feels tasty and expect to get an affirmation.

徐小姐：好吃吧?
Hǎochī ba?
黄小姐：嗯，好吃。
Ǹ, hǎo chī.
徐小姐：我就说好吃嘛。
Wǒ jiù shuō hǎo chī ma.

Miss Xu: Yummy, huh?
Miss Huang: Yes.
Miss Xu: I told you so.

一个音节的句子 One-syllable Sentences
两个音节的句子 Two-syllable Sentences
三个音节的句子 Three-syllable Sentences
四个音节的句子 Four-syllable Sentences

H 4 好吃吗？ Hǎochī ma?

Does it taste good?

询问对方食物的味道好不好。

Used to ask someone whether the food is tasty or not.

徐小姐：好吃吗?
Hǎochī ma?

黄小姐：是羊肉馅儿的饺子吧，我不太喜欢吃。
Shì yáng ròu xiànr de jiǎozi bā, wǒ bù tai xǐhuan chī.

Miss Xu: Does it taste good?

Miss Huang：This dumpling has got a strong smell of mutton, I don't like it very much.

H 5 好冷啊！ Hǎo lěng a!

How cold it is!

感叹很冷。

Used to exclaim that the temperature is too low.

女儿：好冷啊。
Hǎo lěng a.
妈妈：是啊，你多加点儿衣服吧。
Shì a, nǐ duō jiādiǎnr yīfu ba.

Daughter: How cold it is!
Mum: Sure it is. Put on more clothes.

H 6 好美啊！ Hǎo měi a!

How beautiful /Wonderful!

感叹风景、人物等很美。

Used to express something or someone is very beautiful.

徐小姐：好美啊！
Hǎo měi a!
黄小姐：是啊，要不怎么说“桂林山水甲天下”呢。
Shì a, yàobù zěnme shuō “Guìlín shānshuǐ jiǎ tiānxià” ne.

Miss Xu: How beautiful!
Miss Huang: Sure. That's why people always say “East or west, Guilin is the best.”

一个音节的句子 One-syllable Sentences
两个音节的句子 Two-syllable Sentences
三个音节的句子 Three-syllable Sentences
四个音节的句子 Four-syllable Sentences

H 7 好学吗？ Hǎo xué ma?

Is it easy to learn?

询问某种学习活动是否容易。

Used to ask whether something is easy to learn.

约翰：好学吗？
Hǎo xué ma?
乔治：学汉语不太容易。
Xué hànyǔ bù tài róngyi.

John: Is it easy to learn?
George: No. It's not easy for me to learn Chinese.

H 8 喝酒吗？ Hē jiǔ ma?

Want a drink?

询问要不要喝酒。

Used to ask whether somebody wants to have a drink.

小韩：喝酒吗？
Hē jiǔ ma?
小刘：这么久没见了，肯定得喝两杯。
Zhème jiǔ méi jiàn le, kěndìng děi hē liǎng bēi.

Xiao Han: Want a drink?
Xiao Liu: Sure. We haven't met each other for a long time.

H 9 欢迎你。 Huānyíng nǐ.

Welcome.

对对方的到来表示欢迎。
Used to express one's welcome to someone's arrival.

H 10 回去吧。 Huíqù ba.

Let's go back.

提议或劝说对方回去。
Used to suggest that it's time to go back.

丁小宁：回去吧。
Huíqù ba.
林　海：我还想再看会儿。
Wǒ hái xiǎng zài kàn huìr.
丁小宁：不好意思，我先走了。
Bùhǎoyìsi, wǒ xiān zǒu le.
林　海：好的。
Hǎo de.

Ding Xiaoning: let's go back now.
Lin Hai: I want to read for a little longer.
Ding Xiaoning: Sorry. I have to leave now.
Lin Hai: All right. Go ahead!

J 1 集合了。
Jíhé le.

Time for gathering.

叫分散的人聚集到一起。

Used to ask people to get together.

班长：集合了。
Jíhé le.
简萍：我们快走啦，在叫集合呢。
Wǒmen kuài zǒu la, zài jiào jíhé ne.

Monitor: Time for gathering.
Jian Ping: Let's go. Monitor is calling for gathering.

J 2 几点了？Jǐ diǎn le.

What time it is now?

询问当前时间。

Used to ask what time it is.

小韩：几点了？
　　　Jǐ diǎn le?

小刘：快9点了。
　　　Kuài 9 diǎn le.

Xiao Han: What time is it now?
Xiao Liu: Nearly nine o'clock.

J 3 进来吧。Jìnlái ba.

Come in, please.

邀请对方进房间。

Used to invite somebody to come inside a room.

J 4 救命啊！Jiùmìng a!

Help!

表示呼救。

Used to Call for help.

小孩：救命啊！
Jiùmìng a!

小韩：你听，有人喊救命。
Nǐ tīng, yǒu rén hǎn jiùmìng.

小刘：好像在那边。
Hǎoxiàng zài nàbiān.

小韩：走，我们赶紧去。
Zǒu, wǒmen gǎnjǐn qù.

Kid: Help! Help!
Xiao Han: Listen, someone is calling for help.
Xiao Liu: It seems the sound comes from that direction.
Xiao Han: Hurry up! Let's offer him some help.

K 1 开始了？ Kāshǐ le?

Has it started?

询问某项工作（事情、活动等）是否已经在进行。

Used to ask whether something has begun.

小韩：开始了？
Kāishǐ le?

小刘：是，已经开始一会儿了。
Shì, yǐjīng kāishǐ yīhuìr le.

Xiao Han: Has it started?
Xiao Liu: Yes, it has started for a while.

K 2 看书呢？ Kàn shū ne?

Reading?

给正在看书的人打招呼。

Used to greet somebody who is reading.

林　海：看书呢？
Kàn shū ne?
丁小宁：嗯。
Ǹ.
林海：什么书？
Shénme shū?
丁小宁：《红楼梦》。
《Hónglóumèng》.
Lin Hai: Reading?
Din Xiaoning: Yes.
Lin Hai: What book?
Din Xiaoning: *Dream of the Red Chamber.*

K 3 渴死了。
Kěsǐ le.

I am terribly thirsty.

表示自己非常渴，
Used to express that one is terribly thirsty. Here "死了" means one feels very thirsty.

黄小姐：渴死了。
Kěsǐ le.
徐小姐：我这儿有水，你喝点儿吧。
Wǒ zhèr yǒu shuǐ, nǐ hēdiǎnr ba.
黄小姐：谢谢。
Xièxie.

Miss Huang: I am terribly thirsty.
Miss Xu: I got some water here. You can drink it.
Miss Huang: Thank you.

K 4 快点儿走。Kuàidiǎnr zǒu.

Hurry up.

催促对方走快点儿。
Used to urge somebody to walk faster.

妈　妈：快点儿走！
Kuàidiǎnr zǒu！
小孩儿：我脚疼，我走不动了。
Wǒ jiǎo téng, wǒ zǒubudòng le.
妈　妈：乖，小明最听话了。
Guāi, Xiǎo Míng zuì tīnghuà le.

Mum: Hurry up!
Son: My legs ache, I can't move.

L 1

老师好。
Lǎoshī hǎo.

Good day ,teacher.
Hi/hello, teacher.

问候老师。
Used for greeting the teacher.

L 2

老师早。
Lǎoshī zǎo.

Good morning, Teacher.

早上见到老师的问候语。
Used as way of greeting a teacher in the morning.

L 3 累死了。
Lèisǐ le.

I am exhausted.

感叹十分劳累。

Use to express one is extremely tired.

甘玲：累死了。
Lèisǐ le.

简萍：再坚持一会儿，就快到山顶了。
Zài jiānchí yīhuìr, jiùkuài dào shāndǐng le.

Gan Ling: I am exhausted.
Jian Ping: Hold on, we are reaching the top of the mountain right now.

M 1 满意吗？
Mǎnyì ma?

Are you satisfied?

询问对某事物或某人是否满意。

Used to ask someone whether she/he is satisfied with something.

M 2 慢点儿跑。 Màndiǎnr pǎo.

Run slowly.

提醒对方（多为小孩儿）跑慢点儿，注意安全。

Used to remind people (usually children) to run slowly for the sake of safety.

妈　妈：慢点儿跑。
　　　　Màndiǎnr pǎo.
小孩儿：妈妈，您快点儿啊。
　　　　Māma, nín kuàidiǎnr a.
妈　妈：慢点儿，别摔着了。
　　　　Màndiǎnr, bié shuāizhe le.

Mum: Run slowly.
Child: Mum, hurry up!
Mum: Slowly! Be careful!

M 3 慢慢儿走。Mànmānr zǒu.

Mind your steps.

① 送人离开时的客套话。

used as a polite expression to see a visitor off.

黄小姐：慢慢儿走。
Màn mānr zǒu.

徐小姐：不用送了，快回去吧。
Bùyòng sòng le, kuài huíqù bā.

Miss Huang: Mind your steps.
Miss Xu: Thanks. It's very kind of you. Go back your home, please.

② 提醒小孩儿或老人走路慢些，注意安全。

Used to ask the children or the elderly people to walk slowly for the sake of safety.

林海：慢慢儿走。
Mànmānr zǒu.

奶奶：别担心，我腿脚利索着呢。
Bié dānxīn, wǒ tuǐjiǎo lìsuozhe ne.

Lin Hai: Mind your steps.
Grandma: Don't worry about me. My feet are still agile.

一个音节的句子 One-syllable Sentences
两个音节的句子 Two-syllable Sentences
三个音节的句子 Three-syllable Sentences
四个音节的句子 Four-syllable Sentences

M 4 没油了。
Méi yóu le.

The oil has run out.

告诉对方油（汽油、煤油、菜油等）用完了。

Used to tell someone the oil (gasoline or kerosene or cooking oil) has been used up.

妻子：没油了。
Méi yóu le.

丈夫：一点儿都没有了吗？
Yīdiǎnr dōu méiyǒule ma?

妻子：是啊，我正准备做饭呢，真急人！
Shì a, wǒ zhèng zhǔnbèi zuòfàn ne, zhēn jírén!

Wife: The oil has run out.
Husband: Not even a little left?
Wife: No. I am going to cook dinner. What can I do?

M 5 明天见。Míngtiān jiàn.

See you tomorrow.

道别语。

Used as a way of saying goodbye by those who will see each other the next day.

N 1 哪儿上的？Nǎr shàng de?

Which stop did you get on?

询问在哪儿上的车，售票员询问上车地点以便确定票价。

Used to ask the passengers at which stop they got on the bus or train so that the conductor can calculate the price of the ticket.

售票员：哪儿上的？
　　　　Nǎr shàng de?

一个音节的句子 One-syllable Sentences
两个音节的句子 Two-syllable Sentences
三个音节的句子 Three-syllable Sentences
四个音节的句子 Four-syllable Sentences

乘　客：前两个站上的，多少钱？
Qián liǎng gè zhàn shàng de, duōshao qián?

售票员：两块。
Liǎng kuài.

Bus conductor: At which stop did you get on?

Passenger: The second from the last stop. How much?

Bus conductor: 2 Yuan.

N 2 哪种好？ Nǎ zhǒng hǎo?

Which one is better?

面对不同的物品或事物时，希望听话人给予意见。

Used to ask for suggestion from others when one doesn't know which one to choose out of many things.

徐小姐：哪种好？
Nǎ zhǒng hǎo?

黄小姐：全麦的好一些，比较健康。
Quán mài de hǎo yīxiē, bǐjiào jiànkāng.

徐小姐：那就买全麦的。
Nà jiù mǎi quán mài de.

Miss Xu: Which one is better?
Miss Huang: The whole meal bread. It's more nutritious.
Miss Xu: Ok, I will take the wholemeal bread.

N 3 难不难? Nánbùnàn?

Is it difficult?

询问办事情（如考试、做动作等）是不是困难。

Used to ask whether something (an exam or a movement of action) is hard or not.

丁小宁：难不难?
Nán bù nán?
林海：好像不太难。
Hǎoxiàng bù tài nán.

Ding Xiaoning: Is it difficult?
Lin Hai: It seems not.

一个音节的句子 One-syllable Sentences
两个音节的句子 Two-syllable Sentences
三个音节的句子 Three-syllable Sentences
四个音节的句子 Four-syllable Sentences

N 4 你尝尝。 Nǐ chángchang.

Have a taste.

同“尝尝。”
To have the same meaning as “Have a try.”

N 5 你忙吗？ Nǐ máng ma?

Are you busy?

义同“忙吗？”
To have the same meaning as “Busy?”

N 6 你去哪儿? Nǐ qù nǎr?

Where are you going?

询问去什么地方，有打招呼的意思。

Used to ask someone where he is going to, usually as a way of greeting.

林　海：你去哪儿?
Nǐ qù nǎr?

丁小宁：我去图书馆。
Wǒ qù túshūguǎn.

Lin Hai: Where are you going?
Ding Xiaoning: I am going to the library.

N 7 你真好。 Nǐ zhēn hǎo.

It's very kind of you.

夸奖对方好。有表示感谢的意思。

Used to express one's gratitude or to appreciate one's kindness.

徐小姐：你真好。
Nǐ zhēn hǎo.
黄小姐：没什么，我也是举手之劳。
Méi shénme, wǒ yě shì jǔshǒu zhīláo.
徐小姐：那不是没有你的帮助我还真办不成这件事。
Nàbushì, méiyǒu nǐ de bāngzhù wǒ hái zhēn bàn bù chéng zhè jiàn shì.

Miss Xu: It's very kind of you.
Miss Huang: My pleasure. Don't mention it.
Miss Xu: That's a great favor to me. I can't finish it without you. Thanks a lot.

N 8 你是谁？ Nǐ shì shéi?

Who are you?

询问对方的姓名或者身份。
Used to ask the identity or name of someone.

小　韩：你是谁?
Nǐ shì shéi?
快递员：我是送快递的。
Wǒ shì sòng kuàidì de.

Xiao Han : Who are you?
Courier: I am the Courier.

N 9 你瘦了。 Nǐ shòu le.

You are losing weight/
You look much slimmer.

① 告诉对方他的身体消瘦了，表示关心。

Used to tell somebody that s/he looks slimmer in the hope to show one's concern on the him.

小韩：你瘦了。
Nǐ shòu le.

小刘：可能最近比较忙吧。
Kěnéng zuìjìn bǐjiào máng ba.

小韩：你也别光顾着工作，要注意身体啊。
Nǐ yě bié guāng gùzhe gōngzuò, yào zhùyì shēntǐ a.

Xiao Han: You look much slimmer.
Xiao Liu: I am busy these days.
Xiao Han: Don't work too hard.Take good care of yourself.

② 段时间不见，再见面时的寒暄，对女性则带有恭维的意思。

Used as a way of greeting when two friends haven't seen each other for long. If the addressee is a female, that can be a kind of compliment to her.

简萍：你瘦了。
Nǐ shòu le.
甘玲：是么？暑假我经常去锻炼，体重就减轻些了。
Shì me? Shǔjià wǒ jīngcháng qù duànliàn, tǐzhòng jiù jiǎnqīng xiē le.
简萍：难怪身材那么好了。
Nánguài shēncái nàme hǎo le.

Jian Ping : You look much slimmer.
Gan Ling : Am I? I often went to do some physical exercise in the summer vacation, so I lost some weight.
Jian Ping : No wonder you look much slimmer .

N 10 你住哪儿？ Nǐ zhù nǎr?

Where do you live?

询问对方住所。
Used to ask someone where he lives.

小韩：你住哪儿？
Nǐ zhù nǎr?

小刘：我住在北京路十八号。
Wǒ zhù Běijīng Lù shíbā hào.

Xiao Han: Where do you live?
Xiao Liu: I live in the 18th Beijing Road.

N 11 您贵姓？Nín guìxìng?

What is your surname, please?

询问对方姓氏时的敬语。
Used to ask someone what his surname is.

小韩：您贵姓？
Nín guìxìng?

徐小姐：免贵姓徐，叫我徐小姐就是了。
Miǎn guì xìng Xú, jiào wǒ Xú Xiǎojie jiùshì le.

Xiao Han: What is your surname?
Miss Xu: It is Xu. You can call me Miss Xu.

一个音节的句子 One-syllable Sentences
两个音节的句子 Two-syllable Sentences
三个音节的句子 Three-syllable Sentences
四个音节的句子 Four-syllable Sentences

N 12 您几位？ Nín jǐ wèi?

How many people do you have in your group?

询问对方人数。

Used to ask someone how many people there are in his group.

服务员：您几位?
Nín jǐ wèi?
小　刘：三位。给我们一张靠窗的桌子吧。
Sān wèi. gěi wǒmen yī zhāng kào chuāng de zhuōzi ba.
服务员：好的，请跟我来。
Hǎo de, qǐng gēn wǒ lái.

Waiter: How many people do you have in your group?
Xiao Liu: Three. I want a table by the window.
Waiter: Okay. Please follow me.

N 13 您来了？ Nín lái le?

Here comes my distinguished guest/Hello.

对对方的到来表示欢迎。

Used to welcome the arrival of someone.

牛老师：您来了。
Nín lái le.

陈教授：没有想到吧？
Méiyǒu xiǎngdào ba?

牛老师：欢迎欢迎！请进。
Huānyíng huānyíng! Qǐng jìn.

Teacher Niu: Here comes my distinguished guest.

Professor Chen: Didn't you expect I will come?

Teacher Niu: Welcome! Welcome! Please come in!

一个音节的句子 One-syllable Sentences
两个音节的句子 Two-syllable Sentences
三个音节的句子 Three-syllable Sentences
四个音节的句子 Four-syllable Sentences

N 14 您收好。 Nín shōuhǎo.

Please keep it.

提醒对方收存好物品。

Used to remind someone to keep something carefully.

收银员：您收好。
Nín shōuhǎo.

老大爷：好的，谢谢。
Hǎo de, xièxie.

The cashier: Please keep the change.
The old man: Okay. Thank you.

N 15 您填单。 Nín tiándān.

Please fill out the form.

请对方填写收付钱、物的凭据。

Used to ask someone to fill out a form.

业务员：您填单。
Nín tiándān.

小　韩：怎么填啊？
Zěnme tián a?
业务员：这儿有一张样单，您可以照着填写。
Zhèr yǒu yī zhāng yàngdān, nín kěyǐ zhàozhe tiánxiě.

The clerk: Please fill out the form.
Xiao Han: Can you tell me how to fill?
The clerk: Here is a sample. You just follow suit.

N16 您先请。Nín xiān qǐng.

After you!

表示礼让，让对方先做某事。

Used to let someone do something first so as to show one's respect for him/her.

牛老师：您先请！
Nín xiān qǐng!
陈教授：谢谢。
Xièxie.

Teacher Niu: After you!
Professor Chen: Thank you.

一个音节的句子 One-syllable Sentences
两个音节的句子 Two-syllable Sentences
三个音节的句子 Three-syllable Sentences
四个音节的句子 Four-syllable Sentences

P 1 怕什么？ Pà shénme?

What are you afraid of?

询问对方害怕的原因。

Used to ask someone what she/he is afraid of.

林　海：怕什么？
Pà shénme?

丁小宁：我怕旷课的事儿让我爸妈知道。
wǒ pà kuàngkè de shìr ràng wǒ bà mā zhīdao.

Lin Hai: What are you afraid of?

Ding Xiaoning: I am afraid that my parents will get to know that I have played truant.

Q 1 起床了。 Qǐchuáng le.

Get up.

催促对方起床。

Used to urge someone to get up.

妈妈：起床了。
　　　Qǐchuáng le.
儿子：起来了。
　　　Qǐlái le.

Mum: Time to get up.
Son: I'm up, Mum.

Q 2 请给我。 Qǐng gěi wǒ.

Please give it to me.

请求对方把物品给发话人。同“给我”。

Used to ask someone to give something to the speaker himself, with the same meaning as "给我."

一个音节的句子 One-syllable Sentences
两个音节的句子 Two-syllable Sentences
三个音节的句子 Three-syllable Sentences
四个音节的句子 Four-syllable Sentences

Q 3 请过来。Qǐng guòlái.

Please come over here.

请求对方到说话者这边来。同“过来”。

Used to ask someone to come up to the speaker. with the same meaning as “Come here.”

Q 4 请交费。Qǐng jiāofèi.

Please pay the fee.

提醒对方交费。

Used to ask someone to pay the fee.

收费员：请交费。
Qǐng jiāofèi.

小　韩：交多少?
Jiāo duōshao?

收费员：40。
40.

The toll collector: Please pay the fee.
Xiao Han: How much?
The toll collector: 40 Yuan.

Q 5 请买票。Qǐng mǎi piào.

Please buy the ticket.

提醒对方买票。

Used to ask someone to buy a ticket.

售票员：请买票。
　　　　Qǐng mǎi piào.
学　生：请问学生票是半价吗？
　　　　Qǐng wèn xuésheng piào shì bànjià ma?
售票员：对，学生票半价。
　　　　Duì, xuésheng piào bàn jià.

The conductor: Please buy the ticket.
The student: Is the student ticket half-price?
The conductor: Yes, it is.

Q 6 请签字。Qǐng qiànzì.

Please sign your name.

请对方签字。

Used to ask someone to sign his name.

业务员：请签字。
Qǐng qiān zì.
小　韩：签哪儿?
Qiān nǎr?
业务员：这里，谢谢。
Zhè lǐ, xièxie.

The clerk: Please sign your name.
Xiao Han: where?
The clerk: Here. Thank you.

Q 7 请让让。
Qǐng ràngrang.

Please Give me a way.

请求对方让出通道等空间。同“让让。”

Used to ask someone to leave some room in the passage so that the speaker can pass by. It implies “you are in my way.”

Q 8 请入席。Qǐng rùxí.

Please take a seat.

请大家入座，多用在在宴请的场合。

Often used to ask people to be seated in big banquet.

主人：请入席。
　　　Qǐng rùxí.

客人：谢谢。
　　　xièxie.

The host: Please take a seat.
The guest: Thank you.

Q 9 请上车。Qǐng shàng chē.

Please get on the car.

请对方上车。

Used to ask someone to get on the car.

牛老师：请上车。
　　　　Qǐng shàng chē.

陈教授：谢谢。
　　　　Xièxie.

Teacher Niu: Please get on the car.
Professor Chen: Thank you.

Q 10 去哪儿玩儿？ Qù nǎr wánr?

Where shall we go for fun?

询问对方玩耍的地点，有商量的意思。

Used to consult someone where they can go for fun.

林　海：去哪儿玩儿？
　　　　Qù nǎr wánr?
丁小宁：去爬白云山吧？
　　　　Qù pá Báiyún Shān ba?
林　海：嗯，好的。
　　　　Ǹ, hǎo de.

Lin Hai: Where shall we go for fun?
Ding Xiaoning: What about climbing the Baiyun Mountain?
Lin Hai: Good idea.

S 1 上菜吗？ Shàng cài ma?

Shall we serve the dishes to the table now?

询问对方是否可以端菜上桌了。

Used to ask if it is time to serve the dishes to the table.

服务员：上菜吗?
Shàng cài ma?
小韩：再等一会儿，人还没到齐。
Zài děng yīhuìr, rén hái méi dàoqí.
服务员：好的。
Hǎo de.

Waiter: Serve dishes to the table now?
Xiao Han: Wait a moment. Not everyone is here yet.
Waiter: Okay.

一个音节的句子 One-syllable Sentences
两个音节的句子 Two-syllable Sentences
三个音节的句子 Three-syllable Sentences
四个音节的句子 Four-syllable Sentences

S 2

上课了。
Shàngkè le.

The class has begun.

同“上课。”
The same as “Class begins.”

S 3

少喝点儿。
Shǎo hé diǎnr.

Don’t drink too much.

表示规劝对方少喝点儿酒等东西。
Used to persuade someone not to drink too much.

妻子：少喝点儿。
Shǎo hē diǎnr.
丈夫：才喝两杯。
Cái hē liǎng bēi.
妻子：酒喝多了伤身体。
Jiǔ hē duōle shāng shēntǐ.

Wife: Do not drink too much.
Husband: I have had just two cups .
Wife: Drinking too much will do harm to your health.

S 4 谁输了？ Shéi shū le?

Who lost the game?

询问比赛落败的一方是谁。

Used to ask which team has lost the match.

小韩：谁输了？
Shéi shū le?

小刘：哎，曼联队输了。
Āi, Mànlián duì shū le.

Xiao Han: Who lost the game?
Xiao Liu: Ah, Manchester United lost.

S 5 谁赢了？ Shéi yíng le?

Who won the game?

询问比赛获胜的一方是谁。

Used to ask which team won the match.

小韩：谁赢了？
Shéi yíng le?

小刘：皇马赢了。
Huángmǎ yíng le.

Xiao Han: Who won the game?
Xiao Liu: Real Madrid won the game.

S 6 什么病。
Shénme bìng.

What disease?

询问患了哪种疾病。

Used to ask someone what disease s/he suffers from.

S 7 什么茶?
Shénme chá?

What kind of tea?

① 询问茶的品种。

Used to ask the name or brand of the tea.

徐小姐：什么茶?
Shénme chá?

服务员：普洱。
Pǔ'ěr.

Miss Xu: What kind of tea is it?
Waiter: Pu' er.

② 表示对茶的质量或口味不满意。

Used to complain that one is not satisfied with the quality or taste of the tea.

徐小姐：什么茶？
Shénme chá?

服务员：对不起，这茶不合您口味儿吗？
Duìbuqǐ, zhè chá bù hé nín kǒuwèir ma?

徐小姐：是的，请给我换壶好点儿的。
Shì de, qǐng gěi wǒ huàn hú hǎodiǎnr de.

Miss Xu: What kind of tea is it?
Waiter: Sorry. Is this tea not to your taste?
Miss Xu: No, give me a better one.

S 8 生气了？ Shēngqì le?

Are you angry?

询问对方是否生气。

Used to ask whether someone is angry.

甘玲：生气了？
Shēngqì le?
简萍：我才没生气呢。
Wǒ cái méi shēngqì ne.
甘玲：我就知道你没那么小气。
Wǒ jiù zhīdào nǐ méi nàme xiǎoqi.
Gan Ling: Are you angry?
Jian Ping: Am I angry?
Gan Ling: I knew you would not be so petty.

S 9 是谁啊？ Shì shéi a?

Who are you?

同“谁？”
It is the same as “Who?”

S 10 水开了。 Shuǐ kāi le.

The water is boiling.

告诉对方水已经沸腾了。
Used to tell someone that the water has boiled.

S 11 送货吗？ Sòng huò ma?

Can you deliver the goods to my door?

询问对方是否送货，一般出现在买卖活动中。

Used to inquire whether the seller will deliver the goods to the buyer's door.

简萍：送货吗？
Sòng huò ma?

售货员：送货。
Sòng huò.

简萍：请帮我送到北京路110号。
Qǐng bāng wǒ sòngdào Běijīng Lù 110 hào.

Jian Ping: Can you deliver the goods to my door?

Salesman: Yes.

Jian Ping: Please deliver it to the 110th Beijing Road.

T 1

他来吗?
Tā lái ma?

Will he come?

询问某人是否会来。
Used to ask whether someone is coming.

T 2

他是谁?
Tā shì shéi?

Who is he?

询问某人身份。
Used to ask about someone's identity.

白老师：他是谁?
Tā shì shéi?
关老师：新来的李老师啊，你不知道?
Xīn lái de Lǐ lǎoshī a, nǐ bù zhīdao?

Teacher Bai: Who is he?
Teacher Guan: He is the new teacher, Mr.Li. Don't you know that?

T 3 太棒了。Tài bàng le.

Great.

夸赞人、事物、景象等。

Used to praise people, things or sceneries, etc.

简萍：太棒了。
Tai bàng le.
甘玲：是啊，表演太精彩了。
Shì a, biǎoyǎn tài jīngcǎi le.

Jian Ping: Great!
Gan Ling: Yes, the performance is marvelous.

T 4 太吵了。Tài chǎo le.

It is too noisy!

表示声音非常大，嘈杂扰人，一般带有不满的情绪。

Used to complain that the surrounding is very noisy.

小韩：太吵了。
Tài chǎo le.
小刘：是吵，对面的楼房在施工。
Shì chǎo, duìmiàn de lóufáng zài shīgōng.
小韩：真受不了。
Zhēn shòu bù le.

Xiao Han: It is too noisy!
Xiao Liu: Yes, the opposite building is under construction.
Xiao Han: I can not stand it anymore.

T 5 太贵了。Tài guì le.

It is too expensive.

感叹商品价钱太高。
Used to show that the price is too high.

顾　客：太贵了。
Tài guì le.
售货员：先生，这个价钱已经很低了。
Xiānsheng, zhè gè jiàqián yǐjīng hěn dī le.

Customer: It is too expensive.
Salesman: Sir, the price is already very low.

T 6 太热了。Tài rè le.

It is too hot.

意思同"好热。"
It is the same as"好热".

T 7 太险了。Tài xiǎn le.

It was too dangerous./It was really a narrow escape.

① 感叹紧急状况解除了或危险过去了，有侥幸过关的意思。
Used to exclaim over the state of emergency or danger that has passed.

小韩：太险了。
Tài xiǎn le.

小刘：对啊，要不是你急刹车，我们就撞上前面的车了。
Duì a , yàobushì nǐ jí shāchē, wǒmen jiù zhuàngshàng qiánmiàn de chē le.

Xiao Han: It was really a narrow escape.
Xiao Liu: Yes, if you hadn't had emergency brake, our car would have crashed into the front car.

② 表示地形险峻。

Used to mean the landform of a place is very steep.

小韩：太险了。
Tai xiǎn le.
小刘：是啊，我都不敢往山下看。
Shì a, wǒ dōu bù gǎn wǎng shānxia kàn.
小韩：自古华山一条道，山下就是万丈深渊。
Zì gǔ Huà Shān yī tiáo dào, shānxia jiùshì wànzhàng shēnyuān.

Xiao Han: How steep it is.
Xiao Liu: Yeah, I did not dare look down the hill.
Xiao Han: People often say 'There is only one steep way in Huashan'. There is an abyss under it.

T 8 汤咸吗？ Tāng xián ma?

Does the soup taste salty?

询问汤的咸淡。

Used to ask whether the soup tastes salty or not.

妻子：汤咸吗？
Tāng xián ma?

丈夫：不咸不淡，刚刚好。
Bù xián bù dàn, gānggāng hǎo.

Wife: Does the soup taste salty?
Husband: No, it tastes good.

W 1 晚上好。 Wǎnshang hǎo.

Good evening.

晚上的问候语。

Used to greet each other in the evening.

一个音节的句子 One-syllable Sentences
两个音节的句子 Two-syllable Sentences
三个音节的句子 Three-syllable Sentences
四个音节的句子 Four-syllable Sentences

W 2 喂，您好！
Wèi, nín hǎo!

How are you!

打招呼，问候对方。
Used to greet each other in a formal way.

W 3 我爱你。
Wǒ ài nǐ.

I love you.

向对方表达爱恋或深厚真挚的感情。
Used to express one's admiration or affection for someone.

W 4 我饱了。 Wǒ bǎo le.

I am full.

义同“饱了”。
It is the same as“饱了”.

W 5 我存钱。 Wǒ cúnqián.

I want to deposit some money.

义同“存钱”。
The same as“存钱”.

W 6 我干了。 Wǒ gān le.

Cheers.

① 表示自己要将一杯酒喝完。
Used to mean that one will drink up

wine in the glass. This is a way to propose a toast.

小韩：我干了。
Wǒ gān le.

小刘：好酒量。你干了，我也干了吧。
Hǎo jiǔliàng. nǐ gān le, wǒ yě gānle ba.

Xiao Liu: Cheers. Bottom up!
Xiao Han: A greet drinker.Cheers. Bottom up!

W 7 我挂号。 Wǒ guàhào.

I want to register.

告诉挂号员需要挂号。“挂号”是医院为了按顺序给病人看病而对病人进行登记编号。病人看病前先到挂号处交费挂号，然后按编号等候看病。

Used to tell the registrar that one wants to get registered. Registration is a way that the hospital put the patients in order. Patients are supposed to pay the registration fee to get registered in the hospital and then follow the given number to see their doctor.

病　人：我挂号。
　　　　Wǒ guàhào.
挂号员：您挂什么科？
　　　　Nín guà shénme kē?
病　人：外科。
　　　　Wàikē.

Patient: I want to register.
Registrar : Which department?
Patient: The surgical department.

W 8 我困了。Wǒ kùn le.

I am sleepy.

表示自己想睡觉了。
Used to tell someone that one wants to go to bed.

甘玲：我困了。
　　　Wǒ kùn le.
简萍：那你先去休息吧。
　　　Nà nǐ xiān qù xiūxi ba.

Gan Ling: I am sleepy.
Jian Ping: You can go to bed now.

一个音节的句子
One-syllable Sentences
两个音节的句子
Two-syllable Sentences
三个音节的句子
Three-syllable Sentences
四个音节的句子
Four-syllable Sentences

W 9 我取钱。
Wǒ qǔqián.

I want to withdraw some money.

告诉银行业务员自己要把钱取出来。义同“取钱”。
The same as “取钱”.

W 10 我问你。
Wǒ wèn nǐ.

May I ask you a question?

想向对方询问某事。
Used to ask someone about something.

林　海：我问你?
Wǒ wèn nǐ?
丁小宁：什么事?
Shénme shì?
林　海：你知道复习范围吗?
Nǐ zhīdao fùxí fànwéi ma?

丁小宁：不知道。老师说没有范围。
Bù zhīdao. lǎoshī shuō méiyǒu fànwéi.

Lin Hai: May I ask you a question?
Ding Xiaoning: What is it?
Lin Hai: Do you know the scope for review?
Ding Xiaoning: No. Teacher said that all what we have learned should be reviewed.

W 11 我想你。Wǒ xiǎng nǐ.

I miss you.

表示思念对方，一般用于比较亲密的人之间。

Used to express that one misses someone else, generally used between intimate such people as lovers or family members.

一个音节的句子 One-syllable Sentences
两个音节的句子 Two-syllable Sentences
三个音节的句子 Three-syllable Sentences
四个音节的句子 Four-syllable Sentences

W 12 我想吐。Wǒ xiǎng tù.

I feel like vomiting.

表示自己身体不舒服，想呕吐。
Used to show one wants to vomit, meaning that one is not feeling very well as.

黄小姐：我想吐。
Wǒ xiǎng tù.
徐小姐：怎么了？
zěnme le?
黄小姐：胃有些不舒服。
wèi yǒuxiē bù shūfu.
徐小姐：赶紧去医院吧。
Gǎnjǐn qù yīyuàn ba.

Miss Huang: I feel like vomiting.
Miss Xu: What happened?
Miss Huang: I have stomachache.
Miss Xu: Go to the hospital quickly.

W 13 我真背
Wǒ zhēn bèi.

I was so unlucky!

感叹自己不顺，很倒霉。“背”在这里表示“不顺”的意思。

Used to complain that one is very unlucky. Here “背” means ‘unlucky’.

徐小姐：我真背！
Wǒ zhēn bèi！

黄小姐：怎么了？
Zěnme le?

徐小姐：刚买的衣服就被划破了。
Gāng mǎi de yīfu jiù bèi huápò le.

Miss Xu: I was so unlucky!
Miss Huang: What happened?
Miss Xu: My new clothes got scratched by something.

X 1 洗头吗？ Xǐtóu ma?

Do you want to have your hair washed?

询问对方是否要洗头。

Used to ask whether someone wants to have his hair washed in a barber shop.

服务员：洗头吗？
Xǐtóu ma?

徐小姐：不洗。我是陪朋友来剪发的。
Bù xǐ. wǒ shì péi péngyou lái jiǎn fà de.

Baber Shop Assistant: Do you want to have your hair washed?

Miss Xu: No. I just accompany my friend to have her hair cut.

X 2 下雨了。 Xiàyǔ le.

It is raining.

告诉对方正在下雨。

Used to tell people that it is raining.

小韩：下雨了。
Xiàyǔ le.
小刘：是啊，雨还下得不小呢。
Shì a, yǔ hái xiàde bù xiǎo ne.

Xiao Han: It is raining.
Xiao Liu: Yeah, it is raining heavily.

X 3 新年好。
Xīnniān hǎo.

Happy New Year.

新年的问候语。
Used to greet each other on New Year's Day.

Y 1 有空儿吗？
Yǒukòngr ma?

Can you spare me a few minutes?

询问对方是否有空闲。
Used to ask whether someone can.

spare a few minutes to the speaker himself/hersdlf.

小韩：有空儿吗?
Yǒukòngr ma?
小刘：有，你有什么事吗?
Yǒu, nǐ yǒu shénme shì ma?
小韩：想请你帮点儿忙。
Xiǎng qǐng nǐ bāngdiǎnr máng.
小刘：没问题。
Méi wèntí.

Xiao Han: Can you spare me a few minutes?
Xiao Liu: Yes. What for?
Xiao Han: I want you to do me a favor.
Xiao Liu: Sure.

Y 2 有票吗? Yǒu piào ma?

Do you have any tickets left?

询问是否有票。

Used to ask whether there are tickets to sell.

小　韩：有票吗?
Yǒu piào ma?
售票员：有。要几张?
Yǒu. Yào jǐ zhāng?

小　韩：两张。
Liǎng zhāng.

Xiao Han: Do you have any tickets left?
Conductor: Yes. How many tickets do you want?
Xiao Han: Two.

Y 3 有人吗？ Yǒu rén ma?

Is anyone here?

询问是否有人。

Used to ask whether there is a person in a place.

徐小姐：有人吗？
Yǒu rén ma?
小　韩：请问你找谁？
Qǐng wèn nǐ zhǎo shéi?
徐小姐：我找小刘。
Wǒ zhǎo Xiǎo Liú.

Miss Xu: Is anyone here?
Xiao Han: Yes. Who are you looking for?
Miss Xu: I am looking for Xiao Liu. Is he here?

一个音节的句子
One-syllable Sentences
两个音节的句子
Two-syllable Sentences
三个音节的句子
Three-syllable Sentences
四个音节的句子
Four-syllable Sentences

Y 4 有事儿吗？ Yǒu shìr ma?

What can I do for you?

询问对方有什么事。

Used to ask someone if he needs any help.

小韩：有事儿吗？
Yǒu shìr ma?

小刘：我想请你帮个忙。
Wǒ xiǎng qǐng nǐ bāng gè máng.

小韩：没问题。
Méi wèntí.

Xiao Han: What can I do for you?
Xiao Liu: I want you to do me a favor.
Xiao Han: No problem.

Z 1 早上好。 Zǎoshang hǎo.

Good morning!

早上见面时的问候语。

Used to greet each other in the morning.

Z 2 怎么了？ Zěnme le?

What’ s wrong?

向对方询问情况，表示一种关心。

Used to inquire about what is happening to show one’s concern on the addressee.

小韩：怎么了?
　　Zěnme le?

小刘：停水了。
　　Tíng shuǐ le.

Xiao Han: What’s wrong?

Xiao Liu: The water supply has been cut off.

Z 3 真闹心。 Zhēn nàoxīn.

It is quite annoying!

表示心乱、心烦。

Used to show one is upset and annoyed.

一个音节的句子 One-syllable Sentences
两个音节的句子 Two-syllable Sentences
三个音节的句子 Three-syllable Sentences
四个音节的句子 Four-syllable Sentences

徐小姐：真闹心！
Zhēn nào xīn!
黄小姐：什么事儿让你这么闹心啊？
Shénme shìr ràng nǐ zhème nàoxīn ā?
徐小姐：还不是房子的事儿。
Hái bù shì fáng zǐ de shì ér.

Miss Xu: It is quite annoying!
Miss Huang: What makes you so upset?
Miss Xu: It is all about the matter of the house.

Z 4 真热闹。 Zhēn rènao.

How bustling it is!

感叹气氛活跃喧闹、热烈。

Used to exclaim that a place is bustling.

徐小姐：真热闹。
Zhēn rènao.
黄小姐：今天是情人节嘛，街上肯定热闹。
Jīntiān shì Qíngrén jié ma, jiē shàng kěndìng rènao.

Miss Xu: How bustling it is!
Miss Huang: Today is Valentine's Day. Of course the streets is bustling.

Z 5 真是的！Zhēnshì de！

Shit!

表示不满的情绪。

Used to show one's dissatisfaction.

简萍：真是的！
Zhēnshì de！

甘玲：谁又惹你了，让你生这么大的气。
Shéi yòu rě nǐ le, ràng nǐ shēng zhème dà de qì.

简萍：还不是黄红，她自己忘了关灯，被宿管（宿舍管理员）批评，还怪别人。
Hái bu shì Huáng Hóng, tā zìji wàngle guāndēng, bèi sùguǎn (sùshè guǎnlǐyuán) pīpíng, hái guài biéren.

Jian Ping: What a nuisance!
Gan Ling: Who pissed you off and made you so angry?
Jian Ping: It is Huang Hong. She was criticized by the dormitory administrator because she forgot to turn off the lights, but she blamed it on me.

Z 6 真头疼。Zhēn tóuténg.

It is troublesome.

遇到比较麻烦的事或人，表示非常为难或讨厌。

Used to express one's annoyance when encountering troublesome things or people.

小韩：真头疼。
Zhēn tóuténg.

小刘：什么事?
Shénme shì?

小韩：唉，小孩儿上幼儿园的事。
Ài, xiǎoháir shàng yòu'éryuán de shì.

Xiao Han: It is really troublesome.
Xiao Liu: What happened?
Xiao Han: Well, the problem that my child goes to the kindergarten has not been settled down yet.

Z 7 租房吗？
Zū fáng ma?

Want to rent a house?

询问对方是否要出租或租用房子。

Used to ask someone whether she/he wants to rent or lease a house.

中介：租房吗？
Zū fáng ma?

小韩：嗯，想租两室一厅的。
Ǹ, xiǎng zū liǎng shì yī tīng de.

Agent: Do you want to rent a house?

Xiao Han: Yes, I want to rent a house with a living room and two bedrooms.

A 1

唉，我真背。
ài, wǒ zhēn bèi.

Oh, that's tough luck!

义同“真背”。
Used to express the same meaning as ‘真背’.

B 1

把书给我。
Bǎ shū gěi wǒ.

Please give the book to me.

请对方将书交给自己。
Used to ask someone to give the book to the speaker himself/herself.

老　师：把书给我。
Bǎ shū gěi wǒ.
丁小宁：好的，给您。
Hǎo de , gěi nín.

Teacher: Please give the book to me.
Ding Xiaoning: OK, here it is.

B 2 别掺和了。Bié chānhuo le.

Don't get involved in it anymore.

劝告对方不要介入到某些事情中，避免增添麻烦。

Used to advise someone not to get involved in something in order to reduce trouble.

简萍：别掺和了。
Bié chānhuo le.

甘玲：我只是想帮帮他们。
Wǒ zhǐ shì xiǎng bāngbang tāmen.

简萍：只会越帮越忙，你还是别掺和了。
Zhīhuì yuè bāng yuè máng, nǐ háishì bié chānhuo le.

Jian Ping: Don't get yourself involved in it anymore.

Gan Ling: I just want to help them.

Jian Ping: Your help will make things worse, so you'd better keep off the matter.

B 3 别嘟囔了。
Bié dūnang le.

Don't mutter anymore.

劝阻或制止对方不断地小声自言自语，表示不想听。

Used to discourage or stop someone from muttering as one does not want to hear it.

丈夫：别嘟囔了。
Bié dūnang le.
妻子：你不做家务，我说说还不行吗？
Nǐ bù zuò jiāwù, wǒ shuōshuo hái bù xíng ma?
丈夫：行了，你烦不烦啊！
Xíng le, nǐ fán bu fán a!

Husband: Don't mutter anymore.
Wife: You don't do any housework.Can't I make any complaint?
Husband: That's enough.How irritating!

B 4 别吸烟了。
Bié xīyān le.

Stop smoking, please!

阻止或制止对方吸烟。

Used to prevent or stop someone from smoking.

妻子：别吸烟了。
Bié xīyān le.

丈夫：就一支，抽完就不抽了。
Jiù yī zhī, chōuwán jiù bù chōu le.

Wife: Stop smoking, please!

Husband: This is the last one. I won't smoke any more.

B 5 不好意思。
Bùhǎoyìsi.

I am so sorry./ Excuse me.

① 向对方道歉，表示对不起。

Used to make apology to someone.

林海：不好意思。
Bùhǎoyìsì.

甘玲：没关系。
Méi guānxi.

Lin Hai: I am so sorry.
Gan Ling: It doesn't matter.

② 表示打扰了。

Used when one is going to disturb someone.

（甘玲敲林海寝室的门。）
（Gān Líng qiāo Lín Hǎi qǐnshì de mén.）

甘玲：不好意思。
Bùhǎoyìsi.

林海：请进。
Qǐng jìn.

(Gan Ling knocks at the door of Lin Hai's bedroom, and Lin Hai opens the door.)
Gan Ling: Excuse me.
Lin Hai: Come in, please.

B 6 不要吃了。 Bùyào chī le.

Stop eating, please!

劝阻或制止对方不要继续进食。

Used to prevent or stop someone

from continuing to eat something s/he is eating.

甘玲：不要吃了。
　　Bùyào chī le.

简萍：怎么了？
　　Zěnme le?

甘玲：这菜变味儿了，别吃了。
　　Zhè cài biànwèir le, bié chī le.

Gan Ling: Stop eating, please!
Jian Ping: Why?
Gan Ling: This dish has gone sour, so you can't have it.

B 7 不要给我。
Bùyào gěi wǒ.

Don't give it to me.

表示拒绝对方给予的东西。

Used to express one's rejection to accept things given by others.

甘玲：不要给我。
　　Bùyào gěi wǒ.

简萍：是林海托我转给你的，拿着。
　　Shì Lín Hǎi tuō wǒ zhuǎn gěi nǐ de, názhe.

Gan Ling: Don't give it to me.
Jian Ping: It's Lin Hai who asked me to give it to you. Just keep it.

B 8

不要过来。
Bùyào guòlai.

Don't come up to me!

劝阻或制止对方向说话人方向移动。

Used to prevent or stop someone from moving forward to the speaker.

林　海：不要过来！
Bùyào guòlai！

丁小宁：我帮帮你。
Wǒ bāngbang nǐ.

林　海：太危险，别过来！
Tài wēixiǎn, bié guòlai！

Lin Hai: Don't come up to me!
Ding Xiaoning: Let me give you a hand.
Lin Hai: It's too dangerous, so don't come here!

C 1 菜太多了。Cài tài duō le.

There are so many dishes.

就餐时菜的量大、品种多，表示菜吃不完。

Used to show that too many dishes have been made or ordered that they can't be eaten up.

客人：菜太多了。
Cài tài duō le.

主人：哪里，别客气，多吃点儿。
Nǎli, bié kèqi, duō chīdiǎnr.

Guest: There are so many dishes.
Host: You're just being kind. I hope you like them.Just help yourself.

C 2 厕所在哪儿？Cèsuǒ zài nǎr?

Where's the toilet, please?

询问厕所的位置。

Used to inquire about the location of a toilet.

一个音节的句子 One-syllable Sentences
两个音节的句子 Two-syllable Sentences
三个音节的句子 Three-syllable Sentences
四个音节的句子 Four-syllable Sentences

简萍：厕所在哪儿？
Cèsuǒ zài nǎr?
甘玲：直走，前面左转就可以看见了。
Zhí zǒu, qiánmiàn zuǒ zhuǎn jiù kěyǐ kànjiàn le.

Jian Ping: Where's the rest room, please?
Gan Ling: Go straight ahead and then turn left . You can't miss it.

C 3 车太慢了。
Chē tài màn le.

The taxi/bus moves too slowly.

① 速度慢，表示希望车速能够快点儿。

Used to complain the speed of a taxi or bus is too slow in the hope that it can speed up.

林　海：车太慢了。
Chē tài màn le.
丁小宁：是啊，看来我们要迟到了。
Shì a, kànlái wǒmen yào chídào le.

Lin Hai: The taxi/bus goes too slowly.
Ding Xiaoning: Yeah, I am afraid we are going to be late.

② 车的速度不及其它（如飞机）交通工具的速度快，表示出行时不想坐车，而想选择比车快的交通工具。

Used to express one's preference to choose other transportation means(for example airplane) than a car or a train as it takes much longer time to get to a place by them.

小刘：车太慢了。
Chē tài màn le.

小韩：是啊，我们还是坐飞机去吧。
Shì a, wǒmen háishì zuò fēijī qù ba.

Xiao Liu: It takes much longer time to get there by train/bus.

Xiao Han: Yeah, let's go by airplane.

C 4 橙子甜吗？
Chéngzi tián ma?

Does the orange taste sweet?

询问橙子的味道甜不甜。

Used to ask someone whether the orange tastes sweet or not.

甘玲：橙子甜吗?
Chéngzi tián ma?
简萍：嗯，很甜，你尝尝。
Ǹ, hěn tián, nǐ chángchang.
Gan Ling: Does the orange taste sweet?
Jian Ping: Yeah, very sweet. Try some, please.

C 5 吃饭了吗? Chīfànle ma?

Have you had your dinner yet?

询问吃过饭没有，通常是一种见面时的问候。

Used to ask whether someone has already had his/her dinner ,usually as a greeting.

小刘：吃饭了吗?
Chīfànle ma?
小韩：吃了，你呢?
Chī le, nǐ ne?
小刘：吃过了。
Chīguo le.
Xiao Liu: Have you had your dinner yet?
Xiao Han: Yes, and you?
Xiao Liu: Me, too.

C 6 纯棉的吗？
Chúnmián de ma?

Is it made with 100% cotton?

询问衣物等的成份是不是百分之百的棉。

Used to ask whether a clothes are made with 100% cotton.

顾　客：纯棉的吗？
　　　　Chúnmián de ma?

销售员：是的，全棉的。
　　　　Shì de, quánmián de.

Customer: Is it made with 100% cotton?
Clark: Yes, it is.

D 1 打印清单。
Dǎyìn qīngdān.

Please print the list.

请对方打印详细登记有关项目的单子。

Used to ask someone to print the list of the registered items.

顾　客：打印清单。
Dǎyìn qīngdān.
业务员：好的，请稍等。
Hǎo de, qǐng shāoděng.
Customer: Please print the list for me.
Salesman: OK. Wait a moment ,please.

D 2 大家快坐。
Dàjiā kuài zuò.

Sit down, please.

请对方坐下。
Used to ask someone to take a seat.

教　师：大家快坐。
Dàjiā kuài zuò.
同学们：谢谢老师。
Xièxie lǎoshī.
Teacher: Sit down, please.
Students: Thank you.

D 3 大夫，取药。Dàifu, qǔ yào.

Give me the medicine, Sir/Madame.

请药剂师把药交给自己。

Used to ask the pharmacist to give the medicine to the speaker himself/herself.

病　人：大夫，取药。
Dàifu, qǔ yào.

药剂师：什么名字?
Shénme míngzi?

病　人：王红。
Wáng Hóng.

药剂师：给你，吃法都在标签上了，注意看。
Gěi nǐ, chīfǎ dōu zài biāoqiān shang le, zhùyì kàn.

Patient: Sir/Madame, give me the medicine, please.

Pharmacist: What's your name?

Patient: Wang Hong.

Pharmacist: Here you are. Please pay attention to the instruction and it tells you how to take it.

D 4 带伞了吗？ Dài sǎn le me.

Have you brought an umbrella with you?

询问对方有没有带雨伞。
Used to ask someone if he/she has carried an umbrella.

妈妈：带伞了吗？
Dài sǎn le ma?
女儿：带了。
Dài le.

Mother: Have you brought an umbrella with you?
Daughter: Yes.

D 5 当心，有狗。 Dāngxīn, yǒu gǒu.

Be careful with the dog.

提醒对方附近有狗，注意安全，别被狗咬着。

Used to warn someone against the dog nearby.

甘玲：当心，有狗。
Dāngxīn, yǒu gǒu.

简萍：啊，哪里?
Ā, nǎli?

甘玲：就在前边。
Jiù zài qiánbiān.

Gan Ling: Be careful. There is a dog over there.
Jian Ping: Where?
Gan Ling: Just in front of us.

D 6 地铁在哪儿? Dìtiě zài nǎr?

Where's the subway station?

询问地铁的车站在哪里。

Used to ask the location of the subway station.

林　海：地铁在哪儿?
Dìtiě zài nǎr?

丁小宁：过了红绿灯，再向前走100米就到了。
Guòle hónglǜdēng, zài xiàng qián zǒu 100 mǐ jiù dào le.

Lin Hai: Where's the subway station?
Ding Xiaoning: Cross the traffic lights, walk about 100m and you will see it.

D 7 电话通了？
Diànhuà tōng le?

Has the call been put through?

① 询问电话是否接通了。

Used to ask whether the phone has been put through or not.

甘玲：电话通了？
Diànhuà tōng le?

简萍：通了，就是没人接。
Tōng le, jiùshì méi rén jiē.

甘玲：可能没听见吧。
Kěnéng méi tīngjiàn ba.

Gan Ling: Has the call been put through?
Jian Ping: Yes, but no one answered it.
Gan Ling: May be no one was there.

D 8 东西多吗?
Dōngxi duō ma?

Do you have lots of stuff?

询问对方东西是否很多。

Used to ask someone whether he/she has a lot of things or not.

简萍：东西多吗?
Dōngxi duō ma?

甘玲：还好，不太多。
Hái hǎo, bù tài duō.

Jian Ping: Do you have lots of stuff?
Gan Ling: Well, not too much.

G 1 该打针了。
Gāi dāzhōn le.

It's time to have an injection.

提醒打针的时间到了。

Used to remind someone it's time to have an injection.

护士：该打针了。
Gāi dǎzhēn le.

病人：好的。
Hǎo de.

Nurse: It's time to have an injection.
Patient: Okay.

G 2 该您理了。
Gāi nín lǐ le.

It's your turn.

提醒对方可以理发了。
Used to remind someone it's his/her turn to get a haircut.

理发师：该您理了。
Gāi nín lǐ le.
顾　客：好的。
Hǎo de.

Barber: Now it's your turn.
Customer: Thank you.

G 3 赶紧去吧.
Gǎnjǐn qù ba.

Hurry up and go there quickly.

催促对方抓紧时间去某个地方。
Used to urge someone to hurry up.

to go somewhere.

小韩：赶紧去吧。
　　Gǎnjǐn qù ba.
小刘：好的，这就去。
　　Hǎo de, zhè jiù qù.

Xiao Han: Hurry up and go there quickly.
Xiao Liu: Right. Here we go.

G 4 跟你说啊。 Gēn nǐ shuō a.

Listen to me.

说话者提醒对方听自己说，相当于“你听我说件事”。

Used to call the listener's attention when the speaker wants to say something. It has the same meaning as 'I have something to tell you'.

甘玲：跟你说啊。
　　Gēn nǐ shuō a.
黄红：嗯，说吧。
　　Ǹ, shuō ba.

Gan Ling: Listen to me, please. I'll tell you something.
Huang Hong: Well, just tell me what it is.

G 5 功能多吗？
Gōngnéng duō ma?

Does it have a lot of functions?

询问商品的作用多不多。
Used to ask whether a product have a lot of functions or not.

顾　客：功能多吗？
Gōngnéng duō ma?
售货员：功能很多，这种手机还能照相、上网、导航呢。
Gōngnéng hěn duō, zhè zhǒng shǒu jī hái néng zhàoxiàng、shàngwǎng、dǎoháng ne.

Customer: Does it have a lot of functions?
Salesman: Yes, it can be used to take photos, surf the Internet and even navigate the roads.

G 6 恭喜发财。
Gōngxǐ fācái.

Good fortune in the coming year!

祝福语。祝福对方获得大量的钱财。
Used usually on New Years'Day as

greeting to wish someone to have a good fortune in the coming year.

（春节见面。）
（Chūnjié jiànmiàn.）

徐小姐：恭喜发财。
Gōngxǐ fācái.

黄小姐：恭喜发财。
Gōngxǐ fācái.

(When Meeting during the Spring Festival)
Miss Xu: Good fortune in the coming year!
Miss Huang: The same to you!

G 7 恭喜恭喜。Gōngxǐ gōngxǐ.

My congratulations!

祝福语，祝贺对方有喜事。

Used as a greeting to congratulate someone who has some happy thing to celebrate, namely wedding, promotion and the like.

甲：恭喜恭喜。
Gōngxǐ gōngxǐ.

乙：谢谢。
Xièxie.

A: Congratulations!
B: Thank you!

H 1 好点儿了吗？ Hǎodiǎnrle ma?

Do you feel better?

询问对方的状况（心情、情况、疾病等）是否有好转。

Used to ask someone whether his/her mood, condition or health has improved or not.

徐小姐：好点儿了吗？
Hǎodiǎnrle ma?
黄小姐：好多了，头已经不疼了，谢谢。
Hǎo duō le, tóu yǐjīng bù téng le, xièxie.

Miss Xu: Do you feel better?
Miss Huang: Yeah, my headache is gone now. Thank you.

H 2 好久不见。 Hǎojiǔ bù jiàn.

Long time no see!

说话双方已经较长时间没见面了，再见面时的招呼语。

Used as a greeting by people who haven't met each other for a long time.

徐小姐：好久不见。
Hǎojiǔ bù jiàn.

黄小姐：好久不见了，过得怎么样?
Hǎojiǔ bù jiàn le, guò dé zěn me yàng?

徐小姐：挺不错的，你呢。
Tǐng bùcuò de, nǐ ne.

黄小姐：还好。
Hái hǎo.

Miss Xu: Long time no see!
Miss Huang: Long time no see! How's everything?
Miss Xu: Not so bad, and you?
Miss Huang: Everything is OK.

H 3 喝什么茶? Hē shénme chá?

What kind of tea would you like?

① 问对方想喝什么茶。

To ask someone what kind of tea he/she wants to drink.

经理：喝什么茶?
Hē shénme chá?

客户：绿茶吧。
Lǜ chá ba.

Manager: What kind of tea would you like?
Client: Green tea.

② 询问对方正在喝什么茶？

To ask someone what kind of tea he/she is drinking.

徐小姐：喝什么茶？
Hē shénme chá?

黄小姐：普洱。
Pǔ'ěr.

Miss Xu: What kind of tea are you drinking?
Miss Huang: Pu'er Tea.

H 4 合个影吧。 Hé gè yǐng ba.

Let's take a photo together.

请对方与自己一起照相留影。

Used to ask someone to take a photo with the speaker.

甘玲：合个影吧。
Hé gè yǐng ba.

简萍：好的。
Hǎo de.

Gan Ling: Let's take a photo together.
Jian Ping：Okay.

H 5 花(儿)多少钱?

Huār duōshao qián?

How much is this flower?

询问花儿的价格。花（儿），名词，可供观赏的植物。

Used to inquire about the price of the flower. The word “花（儿）” is a noun and indicates an ornamental plant.

顾客：花（儿）多少钱?

Huār duōshao qián?

老板：10元一枝。

10 yuán yī zhī.

Customer: How much is this flower?

Boss: Ten yuan for each.

H 6 花多少钱?

Huā duōshao qián?

How much does it cost?

询问对方花费了多少钱。花，动词，花费、用。

Used to ask someone how much something costs. The word “花” is a verb, meaning “cost”.

徐小姐：花多少钱?
Huā duōshao qián?
黄小姐：花了好几百呢。
Huāle hǎo jǐ bǎi ne.
Miss Xu: How much does it cost?
Miss Huang: Several hundred yuan.

H 7 花(儿)谁送的?
Huār shéi sòng de?

who give the flower to you her/him.

询问花（儿）是谁赠给的。

To ask someone to who give the flower to her/him.

甘玲：花（儿）谁送的?
Huār shéi sòng de?
简萍：我朋友。
Wǒ péngyou.
Gan Ling: Who give the flower to her/himr?
Jian Ping: One of my friend.

H 8 欢迎光临。
Huānyíng guānglín.

Welcome.

欢迎辞，对宾客的到来表示欢迎。
Used to welcome the guests' arrival.

服务员：欢迎光临。
Huānyíng guānglín.
客　人：谢谢。
Xièxie.

Servant: Welcome.
Customer: Thank you.

H 9 回来就好。
Huílai jiù hǎo.

It's fine that you have come back.

告诉对方，他（她）回来了自己就放心。表示对出门在外的人安全归来的欣喜和满足。
Used to express one's relief and happiness when someone else returns safe and sound.

妈妈：回来就好。
Huílai jiù hǎo.

儿子：山体滑坡真吓人，人没砸着，可相机摔坏了！
Shāntǐ huápō zhēn xià rén, rén méi zázhe, kě xiàngjī shuāihuài le!

妈妈：没关系，人没伤着比什么都重要。
Méi guānxi, rén méi shāngzhe bǐ shénme dōu zhòngyào.

Mom: It's fine that you have come back safe and sound .
Son: The landslide was scary. I didn't get injured but the camera broke.
Mom: It doesn't matter. It is the most important that you have come back without being injured.

J 1 几点接送？
Jǐ diǎn jiēsòng?

When shall we pick them up and send them back?

询问接人和送人的时间。

Used to ask when to pick up and send someone back.

小刘：几点接送？
Jǐ diǎn jiēsòng?

小韩：八点在宾馆门口接客人到公司，下午四点半再送客人回宾馆。

Bā diǎn zài bīnguǎn ménkǒu jiē kèrén dào gōngsī, xiàwǔ sì diǎn bàn zài sòng kèrén huí bīnguǎn.

Xiao Liu: What's the time to pick up and send back the guests?

Xiao Han: You should meet the guests at the gate of the hotel at 8:00 am and take them to company .At 4:30pm you send them back to the hotel.

J 2 几点开演？ Jǐ diǎn kāiyǎn?

When does the show start?

询问演出开始的时间。

Used to ask when the show starts.

徐小姐：几点开演？

Jǐ diǎn kāiyǎn?

黄小姐：八点。

Bā diǎn.

Miss Xu: When does the show start?

Miss Huang: At eight o'clock.

J 3 加个菜吧。
Jiā gè cài ba.

Maybe we need one more dish.

增加菜的数量或品种，一般用在担心菜的数量或品种少不够大家享用的时候，有不太确定的语气。

Used to ask whether one more dish is needed when the host is not sure if there's enough food to eat. It's often uttered with uncertainty.

主人：加个菜吧。
Jiā gè cài ba.
客人：不用了，还有这么多菜，都吃不完了。
Bùyòng le, háiyǒu zhème duō cài, dōu chībuwán le.
主人：那好吧。
Nà hǎo ba.

Host: Maybe we need one more dish.
Guest: There are so many dishes that we can't finish them all.
Host: okay.

J 4 叫救护车。Jiào jiùhùchē.

Call an ambulance.

告诉对方赶紧打电话叫救护车。

Used to tell someone to call an ambulance.

甘玲：叫救护车。
Jiào jiùhùchē.

简萍：好的！（拨电话。）喂，120吗，我们这里发生交通事故了，请派救护车。
Hǎo de!（bō diànihuà.）Wéi,120 ma, wǒmen zhèli fāshēng jiāotōng shìgù le, qǐng pài jiùhùchē.

Gan Ling: Call an ambulance.

Jian Ping: Okay. (dialing 120) Hello, is it 120? There's a traffic accident here.Someone got injured. Please send an ambulance.

一个音节的句子
One-syllable Sentences
两个音节的句子
Two-syllable Sentences
三个音节的句子
Three-syllable Sentences
四个音节的句子
Four-syllable Sentences

J 5 今天几号？Jīntiān jǐ hào?

What's the date today?

询问当天的日期。
Used to ask the date.

徐小姐：今天几号？
Jīntiān jǐ hào?
黄小姐：今天12号。
Jīntiān 12 hào.

Miss Xu: What's the date today?
Miss Huang: It's the twelfth.

J 6 今天七夕。Jīntiān Qīxī.

Today is Qixi Festival.

告诉或提醒对方今天是七夕节（中国的情人节）。
Used to tell or remind someone that today is Qixi Festival (Chinese Valentine's Day).

徐小姐：今天七夕。
Jīntiān Qīxī.

黄小姐：你们准备怎样过?
Nǐmen zhǔnbèi zěnyàng guò?

徐小姐：我们准备去看场电影，然后到北京路逛逛。
Wǒmen zhǔnbèi qù kàn chǎng diànyǐng, ránhòu dào Běijīng Lù guàngguang.

Miss Xu: Today is Qixi Festival.
Miss Huang: How will you celebrate it?
Miss Xu: We are going to see a movie and then windowshop around the Beijing Road.

K1 卡被吞了。
Kǎ bèi tūn le.

The card has been swallowed.

银行卡被自动取款的柜员机吞没了，一般是办理业务的人出现被吞卡的情况时向银行说明情况，请求帮助。

Used to ask for help when the credit

cards have been swallowed by ATM.

取款人：卡被吞了。
Kǎ bèi tūn le.

业务员：哦，你保管好回执，明天带上身份证和回执再来办手续取回您的卡。
Ò, nǐ bǎoguǎn hǎo huízhí, míngtiān dàishàng shēnfènzhèng hé huízhí zài lái bàn shǒuxù qǔhuí nín de kǎ.

Customer: The card has been swallowed.
Clerk: Well, you should keep the receipt and come to get your card back with both your ID card and the receipt tomorrow.

K2 快递到了。
Kuàidì dào le.

The express delivery has arrived.

告诉对方快递的邮件到了，表示让对方接收快递的邮件。

Used to tell someone the express delivery has arrived and he/she should come to fetch it.

简萍：快递到了。
Kuàidì dào le.

甘玲：好的，我这就去拿，谢谢。
Hǎo de, wǒ zhè jiù qù ná, xièxie.

Jian Ping: Your express delivery has already arrived.

Gan Ling: Well, I will go to get it. Thank you.

K 3 快来人啊！
Kuài lái rén a!

Help! Help!

呼喊别人来给予帮助，一般出现在遇到紧急、危险等情况时。

Used to ask people for help when one gets into trouble.

简萍：快来人啊！
Kuài lái rén a！
甘玲：来了，来了，怎么了？
Lái le, lái le , zěnme le?
简萍：手被压住了，很疼，快帮我把东西搬开。
Shǒu bèi yāzhù le, hěn téng, kuài bāng wǒ bǎ dōngxi bānkāi.

Jian Ping: Help! Help!
Gan Ling: Here I am. What's the matter?
Jian Ping: My hand was pinned down by something. It's painful. Please help me to move the thing away quickly.

K 4 快没油了。
Kuài méi yóu le.

It's almost out of oil./There isn't much oil left.

① 油不多了，表示车（汽车、摩托车）需要加油了。
Used to show that the vehicle (car, motorcycle and the like) need to fill up fuel.

小刘：快没油了。
Kuài méi yóu le.

小韩：前面就有个加油站，我们到那里加点儿油。

Qiánmiàn jiù yǒu gè jiāyóu zhàn, wǒmen dào nàli jiā diǎnr yóu.

Xiao Liu: It's almost out of oil.

Xiao Han: There's a gas station over there, let's go and fill it up.

② 表示食用油不多了，需要买点儿油。

Used to show that there isn't much cooking oil left and they have to buy some.

妻子：快没油了。

Kuài méi yóu le.

丈夫：我下班后去买点儿。

Wǒ xiàbān hòu qù mǎidiǎnr.

Wife: there isn't much cooking oil left.

Husband: I will go to buy some after work.

K 5 快跑，危险。
Kuài pǎo, wēixiǎn.

Run away quickly.It's dangerous!

提醒和警示对方赶快离开危险地带。
Used to urge someone to leave the dangerous zone at once.

小刘：快跑，危险。
Kuài pǎo, wēixiǎn.
小韩：啊，真险。
Ā, zhēn xiǎn.

Xiao Liu: Run away quickly. It's dangerous!
Xiao Han: My goodness, What a narrow escape.

L 1 来杯咖啡。
Lái bēi kāfēi.

A cup of coffee, please.

告诉对方自己需要一杯咖啡。
Used to tell someone you need a cup of coffee.

徐小姐：来杯咖啡。
Lái bēi kāfēi.
店　员：好的，什么咖啡?
Hǎo de, shénme kāfēi?
徐小姐：拿铁。
Nátiě.
店　员：请稍等。
Qǐng shāoděng.

Miss Xu: A cup of coffee, please.
Waiter: Well, what kind of coffee do you like?
Miss Xu: Latte.
Waiter: Wait a moment, please.

L 2 来多久了? Lái duōjiǔ le?

How long have you been waiting here?

询问对方是否等了很久，有因迟到而感到愧疚的意思。

Used to ask someone whether he/she has waited for a long time, meaning to express one's guilty of being late.

徐小姐：来多久了?
Lái duō jiǔ le?

黄小姐：没多久。
Méi duōjiǔ.
徐小姐：不好意思。
Bùhǎoyìsi.

Miss Xu: How long have you been waiting here?
Miss Huang: Just for a moment.
Miss Xu: I am sorry for keeping you waiting.

L 3 来了，地铁。
Lái le, dìtiě.

Here comes the subway train.

提醒或告诉对方地铁来了。

To remind or tell someone the subway train has come.

简萍：来了，地铁。
Lái le, dì tiě.
甘玲：哦，终于来了。
Ò, zhōngyú lái le.

Jian Ping: Here comes the subway train.
Gan Ling: Oh, it comes at last.

L 4 来一碗饭。

Lái yī wǎn fàn.

Give me another bowl of rice, please.

增加一碗饭，一般用在说话者已经吃了一碗，因没有吃饱，需要再增添饭的时候。

Usually used to mean the speaker needs one more bowl of rice as he/she still feels hungry after having had one.

小　刘：来一碗饭。
　　　　Lái yī wǎn fàn.

服务员：好的。
　　　　Hǎo de.

Xiao Liu: Give me another bowl of rice, please.

Waiter: Okay.

一个音节的句子 One-syllable Sentences
两个音节的句子 Two-syllable Sentences
三个音节的句子 Three-syllable Sentences
四个音节的句子 Four-syllable Sentences

L 5 来瓶啤酒。 Lái píng píjiǔ.

A Bottle of beer, please.

请对方给一支啤酒。

Used to ask the waiter or shop assistant to give him /her a bottle of beer.

客　人：来瓶啤酒。
　　　　Lái píng píjiǔ.
服务员：好，什么啤酒?
　　　　Hǎo, shénme píjiǔ?
客　人：珠啤（珠江牌啤酒）。
　　　　Zhū-pí（Zhū Jiāng pái píjiǔ）.
服务员：请稍等。
　　　　Qǐng shāoděng.

Customer: A Bottle of beer, please.
Waiter: Well, what brand would you prefer?
Customer: Pearl River (Zhujiang Beer).
Waiter: Please wait a moment.

L 6 冷，多穿点儿。
Lěng, duō chuān diǎnr.

It's cold, you should wear more clothes.

天气冷，提醒对方多穿点儿衣服，不要着凉了。
Used to remind someone to put on more clothes so as not to catch cold.

妈妈：冷，多穿点儿。。
　　　Lěng, duō chuān diǎnr.
女儿：哎，我已经加衣服了。
　　　Āi, wǒ yǐjīng jiā yīfu le.
Mom: It's getting cold, put on moreclothes.
Daughter: I have put on more.

L 7 聊什么呢？
Liáo shénme ne?

What are you talking about?

询问聊天的内容或征询对方谈论什么话题，有时也相当于向对方

一个音节的句子 One-syllable Sentences
两个音节的句子 Two-syllable Sentences
三个音节的句子 Three-syllable Sentences
四个音节的句子 Four-syllable Sentences

打招呼。

Used to inquire about the chatting content or topic. Sometimes it functions as a greeting to someone.

甘玲：聊什么呢?
Liáo shénme ne?
黄红：我们正在聊昨晚看的电影呢。
Wǒmen zhèngzài liáo zuówǎn kàn de diànyǐng ne.

Gan Ling: What are you talking about?
Huang Hong: We are talking about the movie we watched last night

L 8 刘先生吗?

Liú xiānsheng ma?

Are you Mr. Liu?

询问对方是不是刘先生。

Used to ask someone if he is Mr. Liu.

徐小姐：刘先生吗?
Liú xiānsheng ma?
刘先生：是的，我是。
Shì de, wǒ shì.

Miss Xu: Are you Mr. Liu?
Mr. Liu: Yes, I am.

L 9 路堵死了。Lù dǔsǐ le.

The road is blocked.

道路因某些原因被阻塞，不能通行。

Used to show that the road is blocked because of some reasons.

小韩：路堵死了。
　　Lù dǔsǐ le.

小刘：真糟糕，我赶时间呢。
　　Zhēn zāogāo, wǒ gǎn shíjiān ne.

Xiao Han: The road is blocked.Traffic comes to a standstill.

Xiao Liu: Terrible/what a nuisanci! I am in a hurry.

M 1 麻烦，点菜。
Máfan, diǎncài.

Excuse me. Please take my order , waiter.

义同“点菜”，“麻烦”客套话。一般用于餐馆、酒店等用餐场合。

It has the same meaning as ‘Please take my order, waiter.’; “麻烦” is a polite way of greetings, which is usually used in restaurants or hotels.

徐小姐：麻烦，点菜。
Máfan, diǎncài.
服务员：好的，请问您要吃点儿什么?
Hǎo de, qǐng wèn nín yào chīdiǎnr shénme?
徐小姐：百合炒西芹、叉烧、还有清蒸鱼……
Bǎihé chǎo xīqín、chāshāo、hái yǒu qīngzhēng yú ……

Miss Xu: Excuse me, Please take my order, waiter.
Waiter: Okay, what would you like to order?
Miss Xu: Sauteed Lily Bulbs and Celery, roast pork and steamed fish…

M 2 麻烦您了。 Máfan, nín le.

Sorry to trouble you!

因请求、拜托对方做某事后所说的一种感谢的话。

It's a polite expression used to show one's gratitude after requesting someone to do something.

徐小姐：麻烦你了！
Máfan nǐ le!

黄小姐：举手之劳，别客气。
Jǔshǒuzhīláo, bié kèqi.

Miss Xu: Sorry to have trouble you!
Miss Huang: You're welcome. It's not trouble at all.

M 3 买点儿什么？ Mǎidiǎnr shénme?

What do you want?

询问对方想买什么物品。

Used to inquire someone what he/she wants to buy.

售货员：买点儿什么？
Mǎidiǎnr shénme?
甘　玲：一瓶牛奶，一个三文治。
Yī píng niúnǎi, yī gè sānwénzhì.
Salesman: Can I help you?
Gan Ling: A bottle of milk and a sandwich.

M 4 买两张票。

Mǎi liǎng zhāng piào.

I want to buy two tickets.

告诉售票员自己需要购买两张票。
Used to tell the conductor that one needs to buy two tickets.

顾　客：买两张票。
Mǎi liǎng zhāng piào.
售票员：两张票一共50元。
Liǎng zhāng piào yīgòng 50 yuán.
Customer: Two tickets, please.
Conductor: Fifty yuan altogether.

M 5 买瓶啤酒。Mǎi píng píjiǔ.

I want to buy a bottle of beer.

告诉售货员自己需要购买一瓶啤酒。

To tell the salesman one wants to buy a bottle of beer.

小　刘：买瓶啤酒。
Mǎi píng píjiǔ.

售货员：好的，什么啤酒?
Hǎo de, shénme píjiǔ?

小　刘：珠啤。
Zhū-pí.

Xiao Liu: A bottle of beer.
Salesman: Okay, what brand do you prefer?
Xiao Liu: Pearl River.

M 6 卖电池吗？

Mài diànchí ma?

Do you sell battery here?

询问商家有没有电池出售。

Used to ask whether or not the shop has battery to sell.

甘　玲：卖电池吗？
Mài diànchí ma?

服务员：有，要几号的？
Yǒu, yào jǐ hào de?

甘　玲：7号的。
7 hào de.

Gan Ling: Do you sell battery here?
Salesman: Yes, what size do you want?
Gan Ling: AAA Battery.

M 7 忙什么呢？

Máng shénme ne?

What have you been busy with these days?

询问对方最近在忙些什么，通常是一种会话开始时候的寒暄。

Used to ask someone what he/she was busy with these days ,usually as a way to start a conversation.

甘玲：忙什么呢?
Máng shénme ne?

黄红：忙着找工作呢。
Mángzhe zhǎo gōngzuò ne.

Gan Ling: What have you been busy with these days?
Huang Hong: I am looking for a job.

M 7 明天有雨。 Míngtiān yǒuyǔ.

It will rain tomorrow.

告诉或提醒对方明天会下雨。

Used to tell or remind someone it will rain tomorrow.

甘玲：明天有雨。
Míngtiān yǒuyǔ.

黄红：真的吗？我得带把伞。
Zhēn de ma？wǒ děi dài bǎ sǎn.

Gan Ling: It will rain tomorrow.
Huang Hong: Really? I have to take an umbrella.

N 1 哪(儿)不舒服? Nǎr bù shūfu?

What's wrong?

询问对方身体有什么地方不舒适。
Used to ask someone what's wrong with him/her.

医生：哪（儿）不舒服?
　　Nǎr bù shūfu?
病人：我喉咙很痛。
　　Wǒ hóulong hěn tòng.
医生：张开嘴，检查一下儿。
　　Zhāngkāi zuǐ, jiǎnchá yī xiàr.

Doctor: What's wrong?
Patient: My throat hurts.
Doctor: Open your mouth and I will give you a check.

N 2 哪个系的。 Nǎ ge xì de.

Which department are you from?

询问对方是什么系的老师或学生。
Used to ask someone which department

he/she belongs to.

白老师：哪个系的?
Nǎ ge xì de?

甘　玲：中文系。
Zhōngwén xì.

Teacher Bai: Which department are you from ?

Gan Ling: Department of Chinese.

N 3 哪(儿)有网吧? Nǎr yǒu wǎngbā?

Where's the Internet bar?

询问网吧所在的位置。

Used to inquire about the location of the internet café.

小刘：哪（儿）有网吧?
Nǎr yǒu wǎngbā?

小韩：我们住的这间宾馆比较偏，附近好像没有网吧。
Wǒmen zhù de zhè jiān bīnguǎn bǐjiào piān, fùjìn hǎoxiàng méiyǒu wǎngbā.

小刘：我去问问前台吧，也许他们知道。
Wǒ qù wènwen qiántái ba, yěxǔ tāmen zhīdao.

Xiao Liu: Where's the internet bar?
Xiao Han: The hotel we stay is remote. I am afraid there is no net bar nearby.
Xiao Liu: I will go to ask the Receptionist. Perhaps they know.

N 4 那是什么？ Nà shì shénme?

What's that?

对自己不了解的事物进行询问。

Used to ask someone what something is.

约翰：那是什么？
Nà shì shénme?

林海：那是风筝。
Nà shì fēngzheng.

John: What's that?
Lin Hai: It's a kite.

N 5 闹什么闹?
Nào shénme nào?

Can't you stop making noise?

要求对方停止吵嚷、玩笑的行为，义同“别闹了”。
Used to ask someone to stop making any noise. It has the same meaning as ‘别闹了’.

N 6 能打折吗?
Néng dǎzhé ma?

Is there a discount?

询问售货员商品能不能降价销售。
Used to ask the salesman whether the product can be sold at a disout.

顾　客：能打折吗?
Néng dǎzhé ma?
售货员：能。打八五折。
Néng. Dǎ bāwǔ zhé.

Customer: Is there any discount?
Salesman: Yes. A fifteen percent discount.

N 7 能上网吗?
Néng shàngwǎng ma?

Does it have an access to internet?

询问计算机能不能连接到互联网。

Used to ask whether the computer have an access to the Internet or not.

林　海：能上网吗?
Néng shàngwǎng ma?

丁小宁：能，就是网速比较慢。
Néng, jiùshì wǎngsù bǐjiào màn.

Lin Hai: Does it have an access to internet?
Ding Xiaoning: Yes, but the speed is rather slow.

N 8 能试穿吗?
Néng shìchuān ma?

May I try it on?

询问衣服或鞋等商品能不能试穿，一般用在购买商品前，想确认该商品是否适合自己。

Used to ask whether the clothes or shoes can be tried on so as to make sure if it is fit for the speaker himself/herself before purchasing it.

顾客：能试穿吗？
Néng shìchuān ma?
店员：可以啊，请到试衣间试穿。
Kěyǐ a, qǐng dào shìyījiān shìchuān.

Customer: May I try it on?
Salesman: Certainly, the dressing room is over there.

N 9 能试试吗？
Néng shìshi ma?

Could I have a try?

询问能不能尝试一下，表示说话人对某一事物感兴趣，想要尝试一下。

Used to ask someone whether something can be tried when the speaker is interested in it and wants to have a try.

顾　客：能试试吗？
Néng shìshi ma?
售货员：能。
Néng.

Customer: Could I have a try?
Salesman: Certainly.

一个音节的句子 One-syllable Sentences
两个音节的句子 Two-syllable Sentences
三个音节的句子 Three-syllable Sentences
四个音节的句子 Four-syllable Sentences

N 10 能刷卡吗?
Néng shuākǎ ma?

Can I pay with the credit/ banking card?

① 询问能否用信用卡或储蓄卡进行购物、消费，一般用在商业消费场所。

Used usually in Commercial Center to ask if one can pay a good or service with credit card, or banking card.

顾　客：能刷卡吗?
Néng shuākǎ ma?
售货员：能。
Néng.

Customer: Can I pay with the credit/banking card?
Salesman: Yes.

② 问能否通过刷卡确认身份。

Used to ask whether one can confirm one's identity by swiping the card.

员工：能刷卡吗?
Néng shuākǎ ma?

保安：不能，对不起，刷卡机坏了，您在这儿签到吧。
Bù néng, duìbu qǐ, shuākǎjī huài le, nín zài zhèr qiāndào ba.

Employee: Can I swipe the card?
Security: No. I am sorry that the Time Attendance Machine was broken. Please sign your name here.

N 11 能转账吗？
Néng zhuǎnzhàng ma?

Do you have transfer services?

询问银行、商业或其它金融机构有没有转账的服务。（“转账”，不收现金，只在双方账户上记载收付关系。）

Used to ask whether the bank, commercial or other financial institutions have transfer service or not. “转账” indicates the bank services of just recording the payment & receipt of the payer and receiver in the banking account ,with no cash being involved.

客户：能转账吗?
Néng zhuǎnzhàng ma?
银行业务员：能。
Néng.
Client: Do you have transfer services?
Bank Clerk: Yes.

N 12 你爸爸呢? Nǐ bàba ne?

Where is your Dad?

询问对方的爸爸在哪里，通常表示说话人想要寻找对方的爸爸。

To indicate that speaker wants to find someone's father by asking where his/her father is.

妈妈：你爸爸呢?
Nǐ bàba ne?
儿子：在书房看书呢。
Zài shūfáng kànshū ne.
Mom: Where's your Dad?
Son: He's reading in the study.

N 13 你多吃点（儿）。
Nǐ duō chīdiǎnr.

Please have more.

劝请对方多吃食物，表示一种礼貌与热情。

Used to ask someone to have more food so as to show one's hospitality.

主人：你多吃点（儿）。
Nǐ duō chīdiǎnr.

客人：谢谢！
Xièxie !

Host: Please have more.
Guest: Thanks.

N 14 你多大了？
Nǐ duōdà le?

How old are you?

询问对方的年龄。

To ask someone's age.

老师：你多大了？
Nǐ duōdà le?

学生：二十岁。
Èrshí suì.

Teacher: How old are you?
Student: Twenty.

N 15 你干吗呀？ Nǐ gànmá ya?

What are you doing?

① 问做什么事。

To ask what he/she is doing now.

妈妈：你干吗呀？
Nǐ gànmá ya?

儿子：我和弟弟捉迷藏呢！
Wǒ hé dìdi zhuō mícáng ne!

Mom: What are you doing now?
Son: I'm playing a game of hide-and-seek with my little brother.

② 表示惊奇，不耐烦、厌恶等情绪。

To express one's surprise or impatience.

林　海：你干吗呀？
Nǐ gànmá ya?

丁小宁：整理书，怎么了？
Zhěnglǐ shū, zěnme le?
林　海：我想再睡会儿，别弄那么大声儿！
Wǒ xiǎng zài shuìhuìr, bié nòng nàme dà shēngr!

Lin Hai: What are you doing?
Ding Xiaoning: I am tidying the books. What's wrong?
Lin Hai: Don't make any noise! I want to sleep for a while.

N 16 你哥哥吗？ Nǐ gēge ma?

Is he your brother?

询问某人是不是对方的哥哥，表示想确认某人的身份。

Used to ask whether someone is the listener's brother in order to make sure his identity.

林　海：你哥哥吗？
Nǐ gēge ma?
丁小宁：不是，他是小学时的同学。
Bù shì, tā shì xiǎoxué shí de tóngxué.

Lin Hai: Is he your brother?
Ding Xiaoning: No, he's my classmate in primary school.

N 17 你家在哪儿? Nǐ jiā zài nǎr?

Where's your home?

询问对方的家庭住址。

Used to ask someone's home address.

老师：你家在哪儿?
　　　Nǐ jiā zài nǎr?
学生：在北京。
　　　Zài Běijīng.

Teacher: Where's your home?
Student: Beijing.

N 18 你教教我。 Nǐ jiāojiao wǒ?

Can you teach me how to do it?

请求对方传授某种知识或技能给自己。

Used to request someone to impart to you some knowledge or skills.

甘玲：你教教我。
　　　Nǐ jiàojiao wǒ.

黄红：好，你先准备棒针和毛线，明天教你（织围巾）。
Hǎo, nǐ xiān zhǔnbèi bàngzhēn hé máoxiàn, míngtiān jiāonǐ（zhī wéijīn）.

Gan Ling: Can you teach me how to do it?
Huang Hong: Okay, you prepare the needle and woolen yarn. I will teach you how to weave a scarf tomorrow.

N 19 你开快点儿。 Nǐ kāi kuài diǎnr.

Drive faster,please.

要求对方加快行驶速度。

Used to ask someone to drive faster.

小韩：你开快点儿。
Nǐ kāi kuàidiǎnr.

小刘：已经60公里（时速）了，市区里再快就超速了。
Yǐjīng 60 gōnglǐ（shísù）le, shìqūlǐ zài kuài jiù chāosù le.

Xiao Han: Drive faster.
Xiao Liu: We are driving around 60 mph, and we are speeding if we drive faster in town.

N 20 你可真行。
Nǐ kě zhēn xíng.

You really are good at this.

① 对对方的言行表示赞赏。
Used to praise one's behavior.

（在学校乒乓球比赛中，丁小宁获得冠军。）
（Zài xuéxiào pīngpāng qiú bǐsài zhōng, Dīng Xiǎoníng huòdé guànjūn.）

黄　红：你可真行。
Nǐ kě zhēn xíng.

丁小宁：没什么，我这次打得比较自信，发挥也正常。
Méi shén me, wǒ zhè cì dǎ de bǐjiào zìxìn, fāhuī yě zhèngcháng.

(Ding Xiaoning has won the champion in the school table tennis contest.)

Huang Hong: You are really good at this.

Ding Xiaoning: It's not a big deal. I was confident ,so I played well.

② 对对方的言行表示讽刺、埋怨。
To express one's complaint or irony for someone's behavior.

妈妈：你可真行。
Nǐ kě zhēn xíng.

儿子：他抢我的东西。
Tā qiǎng wǒ de dōngxi.
妈妈：那也不能打架呀。
Nà yě bùnéng dǎjià ya.
Mom: Aren't you a good boy? You shouldn't fight with him.
Son: He robbed my belongings.
Mom: Even so, you can't fight with him.

N 21 你来点菜。 Nǐ lái diǎncài.

You order the food.

请对方选择菜式，表示客气。一般用于餐馆、酒店等用餐场合。
Used to ask someone to order the food in a restaurant or hotel to show one's modesty.

小刘：你来点菜。
Nǐ lái diǎncài.
小韩：你点吧，别客气。
Nǐ diǎn ba, bié kèqi.
Xiao Liu: You order the food.
Xiao Han：You do it, please.

N 22 （你）来一下儿。(Nǐ) lái yīxiàr.

You, come here, please.

叫对方过来，发话者一般是位尊者或年长者。

Used to ask someone to come to the speaker, who is usually an elderly.

爸爸：你，来一下儿。
Nǐ, lái yīxiàr.
儿子：来了。
Lái le.

Dad: Come here.
Son: Here I am.

N 23 你认识他。Nǐ rènshi tā.

Do you know him?

① 询问对方是否认识某人。

Used to ask someone if he/she knows somebody else

林　海：你认识他？
Nǐ rènshi tā?
丁小宁：认识。
Rènshi.
Lin Hai: Do you know him?
Ding Xiaoning: Yes.

② 对对方认识某人表示惊讶或怀疑。
Used to express one's surprise or doubt that someone should know the other.

妹妹：你认识他？
Nǐ rènshi tā?
姐姐：是啊，他是我的小学同学。
Shì a, tā shì wǒ de xiǎoxué tóngxué.
Younger sister: Do you know him?
Elder sister: Yes, he's my classmate in primary school.

N 24 你是哪儿人？ Nǐ shì nǎr rén?

Where are you from?

询问对方出生、生长的地方。
To ask someone the place where he/she was born & grow up.

一个音节的句子 One-syllable Sentences
两个音节的句子 Two-syllable Sentences
三个音节的句子 Three-syllable Sentences
四个音节的句子 Four-syllable Sentences

白老师：你是哪儿人？
　　　　Nǐ shì nǎr rén?
林　海：上海人。
　　　　Shànghǎi rén.

Teacher Bai: Where are you from?
Lin Hai: I' m from Shanghai.

N 25 你属什么？ Nǐ shǔ shénme?

What's your Chinese horoscope?/ What animal sign were you born under?

询问对方属什么属相，一般可以根据属相来推测对方的出生年份。（"属"，就是以十二属相计生年，"属相"也叫生肖，用十二种动物来标记人的生年。）

Used to inquire under what animal sign one was born. Usually, we can guess people's year of birth according to the Chinese Zodiac. "属" means calculating the year of birth by 12 Chinese zodiac signs. "属相", also called "Shengxiao" marks the year of birth by 12 different animals.

徐小姐：你属什么？
Nǐ shǔ shénme?

黄小姐：属兔。
Shǔ tù.

徐小姐：我属虎，我比你大一岁。
Wǒ shǔ hǔ, wǒ bǐ nǐ dà yī suì.

Miss Xu: What animal sign were you born under?/What's your Chinese horoscope?
Miss Huang: I'm a Rabbit in the Chinese horoscope.
Miss Xu: I'm a Tiger, so I am one year older than you.

N 26 你要什么？ Nǐ yào shénme?

What do you want?

询问对方希望得到什么。

To ask someone what he or she wants to have.

妈妈：你要什么？
Nǐ yào shénme?

儿子：蛋糕。
Dàngāo.

Mum: What do you want?
Son: I want cake.

N 27 你怎么了？ Nǐ zěnme le?

What's the matter with you?

看到对方的身体或精神状况异常，询问对方的状况。

Used to ask someone's health condition when seeing he/she is not feeling well.

简萍：你怎么了？
　　　Nǐ zěnme le?
黄红：胃不舒服。
　　　Wèi bù shūfu.
简萍：我陪你去医务室看看吧。
　　　Wǒ péi nǐ qù yīwùshì kànkan ba.

Jian Ping: What's the matter with you?
Huang Hong: Something's wrong with my stomach
Jiang Ping: let me accompany you to the clinic.

N 28 你住几楼？ Nǐ zhù jǐ lóu?

Which floor do you live on?

询问对方住在哪一层楼。

Used to inquire someone which floor he/she lives on.

小韩：你住几楼？
　　　Nǐ zhù jǐ lóu?

小刘：我住在三楼。
　　　Wǒ zhù zài sān lóu.

Xiao Hai: Which floor do you live on?
Xiao Liu: I'm on the second floor.

N 29 您吃什么？ Nín chī shénme?

What would you like?

就餐前，询问对方喜欢或想要吃什么食物、菜式，表示一种礼貌和尊重。

Used (usually before dinner) to ask someone what he / she likes to have so as to express one's politeness and respect to the addressee.

女儿：您吃什么？
Nín chī shénme?
爸爸：面包和牛奶就可以了。
Miànbāo hé niúnǎi jiù kěyǐ le.

Daughter: What would you like?
Father: Bread and milk will be ok.

N 30 您好，老师。
Nín hǎo, lǎoshī.

Hello, teacher!

对老师的问候语。
Used as greeting to teachers, having the same meaning as "老师，您好！".

N 31 您喝茶吗？
Nín hé chā ma?

Would you like to have some tea?

询问对方是否愿意喝茶。
Used to ask someone whether he or

she wants some tea.

白老师：您喝茶吗?
Nín hē chá ma?

陈教授：不喝茶，白开水就可以，谢谢。
Bù hē chá, báikāishuǐ jiù kěyǐ, xièxie.

Teacher Bai: Would you like to have some tea?

Professor Chen: No tea. Water will be fine. Thank you.

N 32 您剪发吗? Nín jiǎnfà ma?

Do you want to have your hair cut?

在发廊或美发店，店员询问顾客是否需要剪头发。

Used in the hair salon by the assistants to ask whether a customer would like to have a haircut.

店员：您剪发吗?
Nín jiǎnfà ma?

顾客：剪发。
Jiǎnfā.

Assistant: Do you want to have your hair cut?

Customer: Yes.

N 33 您辛苦了。 Nín xīnkǔ le.

You have worked hard!/Thanks for your hard work.

对对方做出的工作与努力表示肯定、赞扬，有时也表示客套。

Used sometimes just as politeness of manner to express one's praise or admiration to someone's hard work and effort,.

家长：您辛苦了。
Nín xīnkǔ le.

老师：这是我应该做的。
Zhè shì wǒ yīnggāi zuò de.

Parents: Thanks for your hard work.
Teacher: My pleasure/The pleasure is mine.

N 34 您要多少？
Nín yào duōshao?

How many/much do you need?

在商品交易时，售卖商品的一方询问顾客需要商品的数量，有时也用在其他一些给人提供物品的场合。

Used by the sellers to ask the quantity of the goods the customer needs.

店员：您要多少？
Nín yào duōshao?

顾客：两斤。
Liǎng jīn.

Assistant: How much do you need?
Customer: One kilogram.

N 35 您做衣服？ Nín zuò yīfu?

Do you want to make clothes?

裁缝师傅询问顾客是否需要做衣服。

Used by the tailors to ask whether one needs to make clothes.

裁缝：您做衣服？
Nín zuò yīfu?
顾客：是，我想做旗袍。
Shì, wǒ xiǎng zuò qípáo.

Tailor: Do you want to make clothes?
Customer: Yes, I want cheongsam.

N 36 您坐这儿。 Nín zuò zhèr.

Sit here, please.

示意对方坐在某个位子上。

Used to signal someone to sit in certain seat.

服务员：您坐这儿。
Nín zuò zhèr.
顾　客：谢谢。
Xièxie.
Assistant: Sit here, please.
Customer: Thank you.

N 37 牛奶有吗？
Niúnǎi yǒu ma?

Do you have milk?

义同"有牛奶吗"。
Used to express the same meaning as "Is there any milk?"

P 1 便宜点儿。
Piányi dianr.

Can it be cheaper?

在商品交易时，买卖双方进行讨价还价，买方要求卖方降低商品的价格。

Used by the buyers to ask for lower the price of goods.

顾　客：便宜点儿?
Piányi diǎnr?

售货员：价钱已经很低了，不能再便宜了。
Jiàqián yǐjīng hěn dī le, bùnéng zài piányi le.

Customer: Can it be cheaper?

Assistant: The price is already quite low.It cannot be any lower.

Q 1 起疹子了。 Qǐ zhěnzi le.

Have a rash?

询问皮肤表面是否出现小疙瘩了，“疹子”是麻疹的通称。

Used to ask whether there are any rash on someone's skin. “Rash” is a general term for “measles”.

妈妈：起疹子了?
Qǐ zhěnzi le?

女儿：是，一大片，很痒！
Shì, yī dà piàn, hěn yǎng!

妈妈：先擦点儿皮炎平，我们这就去医院。
Xiān cādiǎnr píyánpíng, wǒmen

zhè jiù qù yīyuàn.

Mum: Have some rash?

Daughter: Yes, a big patch. It is very itching.

Mum: Rub this medicine (Compound Dexamethasone Acetate Cream)on it .Let's go to the hospital.

Q2 气色不错。 Qìsè bùcuò.

You look good.

称赞他人身体与精神状态好。（“气色”，人的精神状态和健康状况在面部的表现。）

Used to praise someone who is in good health and high spirit. “气色” indicates good complexion.

小韩：气色不错。
Qìsè bùcuò.

小刘：哦，是吗？大概是这几天休息好了。
Ò, shì ma? dàgài shì zhè jǐ tiān xiūxi hǎo le.

小韩：是你人逢喜事精神爽吧。
Shì nǐ rén féng xǐshì jīngshén shuǎng ba.

Xiao Han: You look good.
Xiao Liu: Oh, really? I guess it is because I have had a good rest these days.
Xiao Han: Maybe you must have had something good to celebrate.

Q 3 请按5楼。
Qǐng àn 5 lóu.

Press five, please.

请对方帮忙按下电梯上的数字按键“5”，表示电梯到5楼需要停一下。

Used to ask someone to press the number 5 on the number pad of the elevator, which means one needs to go to the fifth floor.

黄红：请按5楼。
Qǐng àn 5 lóu.
（林海帮忙按下5楼的数字按键。）
（Lín Hǎi bāngmáng ànxià 5 lóu de shùzi ànjiàn.）

黄红：谢谢。
Xièxie.

Huang Hong: Press five, please.
(Lin Hai helps to press the number five on the number pad.)
Huang Hong: Thank you.

Q 4 请别客气。Qǐng bié kèqi.

Make yourself at home, please./Get yourself relaxed.

在招待他人时，希望对方随便一点儿，不要太拘束。
Used by the host to ask the guests to get relaxed when hosting them at his home.

主人：请别客气。
Qǐng bié kèqi.
客人：谢谢。
Xièxie.

Host: Make yourself at home, please./Get yourself relaxed.
Guest: Thanks.

一个音节的句子 One-syllable Sentences
两个音节的句子 Two-syllable Sentences
三个音节的句子 Three-syllable Sentences
四个音节的句子 Four-syllable Sentences

Q5 请多关照。
Qǐng duō guānzhào.

Wish you to give me more care & help.

请求对方照顾、帮助自己，常用于说话人到新的地方或认识新的人时，表示一种谦虚和诚恳的态度。

Used to ask for help and care, usually to show one's modesty and sincerity when coming to a new environment or making new friends.

新员工：请多关照。
Qǐng duō guānzhào.
老员工：请多关照。
Qǐng duō guānzhào.

New employee: Wish you give me more care and help.
Senior employee: Me too.

Q6 请多指教。
Qǐng duō zhǐjiào.

Please give me more advice!

请求对方对自己提供帮助和指导。

Used to ask for advice or show one's modesty.

新员工：请多指教。
Qǐng duō zhǐjiào.

老员工：别客气，互相学习。
Bié kèqi, hùxiāng xuéxí.

New employee: Please give me more advice!

Senior employee: You are welcome. We can learn from each other.

Q7 请喝咖啡。
Qǐng hē kāfēi.

Have some coffee, please.

招待对方饮用咖啡。

Used to treat someone with coffee.

主人：请喝咖啡。
　　　Qǐng hē kāfēi.
客人：谢谢。
　　　Xièxie.

Host: Have some coffee, please.
Guest: Thank you.

Q 8 请教练吗？
Qǐng jiàoliàn ma?

Do you want to get a coach?

询问是否需要聘请教练指导，一般用在健身房或其他运动场所。

Used in the gym or other sports center to ask whether one needs a coach.

服务员：请教练吗？
　　　Qǐng jiàoliàn ma?
小　刘：请，1小时多少钱。
　　　Qǐng, 1 xiǎoshí duōshao qián.
服务员：单个儿辅导，100块；一对多辅导，10块。
　　　Dāngèr fǔdǎo,100 kuài; yī duì duō fǔdǎo,10 kuài.

Waiter: Do you want to get a coach?
Xiao Liu: Yes, how much for one hour?
Waiter: 100RMB for one to one coach;
　　　10RMB for one to many coach.

Q 9 请快点儿。Qǐng kuài diǎnr.

Hurry up, please.

礼貌地催促对方加快速度。

To urge politely someone to do things more quickly.

乘务员：请快点儿。
　　　　Qǐng kuàidiǎnr.

乘　客：好的。
　　　　Hǎo de.

乘务员：列车马上就要开了。
　　　　Lièchē mǎshàng jiùyào kāi le.

Train Conductor: Hurry up, please.

Passenger: Ok.

Train Conductor: The train is leaving soon.

Q 10 请签个名儿。Qǐng qiān ge míngr.

Please sign your name here.

请求对方在相应的地方写上自己的名字。

Used to ask someone to write down his or her name in corresponding place.

观众：请签个名儿。
Qǐng qiān gè míngr.
歌星：好的。
Hǎo de.
观众：谢谢。
Xièxie.

Audience: Please sign your name here.
Singer: Ok.
Audience: Thanks.

Q 11 请让个座儿。Qǐng ràng gè zuòr.

Please give your seat to him/her.

在某些公共场合（如公交车、地铁等），要求对方把座位给有特殊需要的人（如老人、小孩儿、孕妇等）。

Used in some public places(like bus, subway train and so on) to ask someone to offer their seats to other passengers (like the elderly, kids and the pregnant women) who is in greater need of them.

司机：请让个座儿。

Qǐng ràng gè zuòr.

乘客：好，老奶奶您坐这儿。

Hǎo, lǎo nǎinai nín zuò zhèr.

老奶奶：谢谢！

Xièxie !

The driver: Please give your seat to this lady.

Passenger: Sure. Please sit down.

The old lady: Thank you !

Q 12 请先存包。

Qǐng xiān cún bāo.

Please deposit your bag first.

在某些场合（如超市、考场等）出于管理和服务的需要，说话者要求对方把携带的袋子存放在指定的地方，不带入场内。

Used by the speaker to ask people to put their bags in a given place without bringing them in the supermarket or examination room.

店员：请先存包。
Qǐng xiān cún bāo.
顾客：好。包儿存在哪里?
Hǎo. bāor cún zài nǎli?
店员：左边直走，有个寄存处。
Zuǒ biān zhí zǒu, yǒu gè jì cúnchù.
顾客：谢谢。
Xièxie.

Assistant: Please deposit your bag.
Customer: Ok. Where shall I put the bag?
Assistant: Go straight on the left and you' u see a checkroom.

Q 13 请这边坐。 Qǐng zhè biān zuò.

Please sit here.

引导、告知对方坐到相应的座位上。

Used to tell people to sit down at certain seat.

（电影放映厅。）
（Diànyǐng fàngyìngtīng.）
引导员：请这边坐。
Qǐng zhè biān zuò.

观　众：谢谢。
Xièxie.

（In the theatre.）
Usher: Please sit down here.
Audience: Thank you.

Q 14 去逛街吗？
Qù guàngjiē ma?

Would you like to go shopping with me?

询问对方是否要去逛街。

Used to ask people whether he or she wants to go shopping with the speaker.

简萍：去逛街吗？
Qù guàngjiē ma?
黄红：去，准备下午去逛。
Qù, zhǔnbèi xiàwǔ qù guàng.

Jian Ping: Would you like to go shopping with me?
Huang Hong: Yes. I want to go shopping this afternoon.

Q 15 去哄哄他。

Qù hónghong tā.

Just go to amuse him.

当某人生气、失望或伤心时，希望对方去哄逗这个人变得平静或开心一点儿。

Used to let one make someone else cheer up when he/she gets angry, disappointed or upset.

简萍：去哄哄她。
Qù hǒnghong tā.

黄红：都是你弄得她不开心，现在又让我来哄。
Dōu shì nǐ nòngde tā bù kāixīn, xiànzài yòu ràng wǒ lái hǒng.

简萍：你就哄哄她吧，谢了。
Nǐ jiù hǒnghong tā ba, xiè le.

黄红：我试试看。
Wǒ shìshi kàn.

Jian Ping: Just go to amuse her.

Huang Hong: It's you who make her unhappy. Now you should let me amuse her.

Jian Ping: I didn't know she care so much about it. Please just go to amuse her. Thank you.

Huang Hong: Let me try.

R 1 人真多啊。 Rén zhēn duō a.

There are so many people.

① 感叹某一场所人很多。

Used to exclaim there is many people in some place.

小刘：人真多啊！
Rén zhēn duō a！

小韩：是啊，真热闹！
Shì a, zhēn rènao！

Xiao Liu: There are so many people!
Xiao Han: Yes, it is quite bustling.

R 2 认识一下儿。 Rènshi yīxiàr.

Introduce you to each other.

帮助介绍人们彼此之间互相认识。

Used to introduce people to get to know each other.

小 韩：认识一下儿。
Rènshi yīxiàr.

徐小姐：你好，我姓徐。
Nǐ hǎo, wǒ xìng Xú.
小　刘：我姓刘，叫我小刘就可以了。
Wǒ xìng Liú, jiào wǒ Xiǎo Liú jiù kěyǐ le.

Xiao Hai: Introduce you to each other.
Miss Xu: Hello, My family name is Xu.
Xiao Liu: Hello,Xu. My family name is Liu. You can call me Xiao Liu.

S 1 商量个事（儿）。
Shāngliang gè shìr.

I want to discuss a thing with you.

表示说话人想要与对方讨论、沟通某件事情。

Used to indicate the speaker wants to discuss a thing with someone.

小韩：商量个事（儿）。
Shāngliang gè shìr.
小刘：什么事儿？您说。
Shénme shìr？Nín shuō.

Xiao Han: I want to discuss a thing with you.
Xiao Liu: What's up? Just say it.

S 2 少喝点（儿）酒。
Shǎo hēdiǎnr jiǔ.

Don't drink too much wine.

出于关心，劝说对方要少饮酒。

Used to persuade someone not to drink too much wine in order to show one's concern for him/ her.

妻子：少喝点（儿）酒。
Shǎo hēdiǎnr jiǔ.

丈夫：知道啦。
Zhīdao la.

Wife: Don't drink too much wine.
Husband: I see.

S 3 谁和谁比？
Shéi hé shéi bǐ?

Which two teams are playing?

询问比赛、较量的双方是什么人或代表队。

To ask which two teams are playing.

小刘：谁和谁比？
Shéi hé shéi bǐ?
小韩：中国队和美国队比。
Zhōngguó Duì hé Měiguó Duì bǐ.
Xiao Liu: Which two teams are playing?
Xiao Han: Chinese Team with American Team.

S 4 谁是经理？ Shéi shì jīnglǐ?

Who is the manager?

询问经理是哪个人。
Used to ask who the manager is.

徐小姐：谁是经理？
Shuí shì jīnglǐ?
经理：我就是，请问有什么事？
Wǒ jiùshì, qǐng wèn yǒu shénme shì?
Miss Xu: Who is the Manager?
Manager: It's me.What's up?

S 5 生日快乐！ Shēngrì kuàilè！

Happy birthday!

祝福语，给对方的生日祝福。

Used as blessings to celebrate one's birthday.

简萍：生日快乐！
Shēngrì kuàilè！

甘玲：谢谢！
Xièxie！

Jian Ping: Happy birthday!
Gan Ling: Thank you.

S 6 试一下吧。 Shì yīxià ba.

Have a try.

希望或劝说对方尝试一下儿。

Used to persuade someone to have a try.

林海：试一下吧。
Shì yīxià ba.

黄红：好啊，我试试。
Hǎo a, wǒ shìshi.

Lin Hai: Have a try.
Huang Hong: Ok. Let me try it now.

S 7 受不了了。
Shòubùliǎo le.

I can't stand it anymore.

抱怨、感慨不能忍受某人、某事物或承受某种痛苦。

Used to complain one cannot stand with someone, something or some suffering.

姐姐：受不了了。
Shòubùliǎo le.

妹妹：我唱歌有那么难听吗?
Wǒ chànggē yǒu nàme nántīng ma?

姐姐：你练好了再唱吧，跑调儿了！
Nǐ liàn hǎole zài chàng ba, pǎodiàor le!

Elder sister: I can't stand it anymore. It sounds terrible.
Young sister: Is my singing so awful?
Elder sister: You'd better sing after more practice. It's out of tune.

S 8 睡个好觉。
Shuì gè hǎo jiǎo.

Have a good sleep.

常用于临睡前，表示问候或道别的话语。

Used as a greeting or as a way to say good-bye before going to bed.

徐小姐：睡个好觉。
Shuì gè hǎo jiào.

黄小姐：晚安。
Wǎn'ān.

Miss Xu: Have a good sleep.
Miss Huang: Good night.

T 1 他喝醉了。
Tā hē zuì le.

He is drunk.

表示某人饮酒过量，一般用于阻拦敬酒或解释醉酒后的行为。

Used to describe someone who has drunk too much so as to prevent more toast to him/her or explain one's abnormal actions after getting drunk.

小韩：他喝醉了。
Tā hē zuì le.

小刘：喝成这样了，我送他回家吧。
Hēchéng zhèyàng le, wǒ sòng tā huíjiā ba.

Xiao Han: He is drunk.
Xiao Liu: He is so drunk. I'd better send him back home.

T 2 他是刘明。Tā shì Lí Míng.

He is Liu Ming.

介绍、告知他人的姓名。

Used to introduce a person's name.

小韩：他是刘明。
Tā shì Liú Míng.

徐小姐：你好，刘明。我姓徐。
Nǐ hǎo, Liú Míng. wǒ xìng Xú.

刘明：你好，徐小姐。
Nǐ hǎo, Xú Xiǎojie.

Xiao Han: He is Liu Ming.
Miss Xu: Hello, Liu Ming. My family name is Xu.
Liu Ming: Hi, Miss Xu.

T 3 他太懒了。 Tā tài lǎn le.

He is too lazy.

表示某人行为懒惰，有不满、指责和厌恶的意思。

Used to complain or accuse someone of his laziness.

林　海：他太懒了。
　　Tā tài lǎn le.

丁小宁：是啊，臭袜子不洗还到处扔，弄得宿舍臭烘烘的。
　　Shì a, chòu wàzi bùxǐ hái dàochǔ rēng, nòngde sùshè chòu hōnghōng de.

Lin Hai: He is too lazy.

Ding Xiaoning: Yes, he didn't wash his socks and threw them everywhere. The dormitory smells bad.

T4 他太贪了。
Tā tài tān le.

He is too greedy.

表示某人贪婪，有指责、不满和厌恶的意思。

Used to complain someone is greedy.

小韩：他太贪了。
Tā tài tān le.

小刘：是啊，不然他也不会被关（被关在监狱）这么久。
Shì a, bùrán tā yě bùhuì bèi guān（bèi guān zài jiānyù）zhème jiǔ.

Xiao Han: He is too greedy.

Xiao Liu: Yes, or he would not be put into prison for so long.

T5 她挺好的。
Tā tíng hǎo de.

She is kind.

对某人身体状况或人品、性格等做出的好的评价。

Used to praise someone's physical

state, character or personality.

徐小姐：她挺好的。

Tā tǐng hǎo de.

黄小姐：是啊，我也挺喜欢她的。

Shì a, wǒ yě tǐng xǐhuan tā de.

Miss Xu: She is kind.

Miss Huang: Yes, I like her very much.

T 6 他挺帅的。 Tā tǐng shuài de.

He is handsome/smart.

评价某人长得漂亮或言行潇洒，一般用于对男士评价。

Used to praise a man's good appearance and behaviors.

简萍：他挺帅的。

Tā tǐng shuài de.

甘玲：我也觉得他挺帅的，你觉不觉得他长得像言承旭?

Wǒ yě juéde tā tǐng shuài de, nǐ juébùjuéde tā zháng de xiàng Yán Chéngxù?

简萍：嗯，很像。

Ǹ, hěn xiàng.

Jian Ping: He is handsome/smart.

Gan Ling: I think so. Don't you think he looks like Jerry Yan?

Jian Ping: Yes, He's quite like him.

T 7 她又胖了。
Tā yòu pàng le.

She is putting on weight.

表示某人比原来更胖了。

Used to mean someone looks fatter than before.

简萍：她又胖了。
Tā yòu pàng le.

黄红：是啊，一个假期她又胖了很多。
Shì a, yī gè jiǎqī tā yòu pàngle hěnduō.

Jian Ping: She is putting on some weight.

Huang Hong: Yes, her weight is out of control after the vacation.

T 8 她长癣了。
Tā zhāng xuǎn le.

She has had tinea.

告知某人得了"癣"这种皮肤病。"癣"是常见皮肤病的总称。

Used to tell her that she has got

tinea, a kind of skin disease. "癣" is the general term for ordinary skin disease.

简萍：她长癣了。
Tā zháng xuǎn le.

黄红：那要注意了。
Nà yào zhùyì le.

Jian Ping: She has had tinea.
Huang Hong: She must be careful with it.

T 9 太高兴了。Tài gāoxìng le.

I'm so glad!

表达自己非常愉悦、兴奋的心情。
Used to express someone is really happy.

杰克：太高兴了！
Tai gāoxìng le！

约翰：是啊，你汉语水平考试的成绩那么好，我也为你高兴！
Shì a, nǐ Hànyǔ Shuǐpíng Kǎoshì de chéngjì nàme hǎo, wǒ yě wèi nǐ gāoxìng！

Jack: I'm so glad!
John: Sure, your HSK achievement is excellent. I am glad for you, too.

T 10 太过分了。 Tài guòfèn le.

That's going a bit too far.

指责某人的行为，表示极度不满。（"过分"，形容超过了某个范围或限度。）

Used to complain someone's behavior has gone beyond the limit. "过分" means "beyond the limit" "going too far".

林　海：太过分了。
Tài guòfèn le.

丁小宁：是太过分了！明知道大家在午休还把电脑的声音弄得那么大。
Shì tài guòfèn le! míng zhīdao dàjiā zài wǔxiū hái bǎ diànnǎo de shēngyīn nòng de nàme dà.

Lin Hai: That's going a bit too far.

Ding Xiaoning: It is really too much. He knew we are taking a nap after lunch, but he still make his computer so noisy.

T 11 太精彩了。 Tài jīngcǎi le.

It's wonderful!

对某个活动、表演或作品表示肯定和赞扬。

Used to praise an activity, performance or work.

杰克：太精彩了！
Tài jīngcǎi le！

约翰：京剧真让人着迷。
Jīngjù zhēn ràng rén zháomí.

Jack: It's wonderful!
John: Beijing Opera is fascinating.

T 12 太可怕了。 Tài kěpà le.

It is horrible!

听说或遇到危险时，感到恐惧之后的评价与感叹。

Used to show one's fear when having encountered or been told something

一个音节的句子 One-syllable Sentences
两个音节的句子 Two-syllable Sentences
三个音节的句子 Three-syllable Sentences
四个音节的句子 Four-syllable Sentences

extremely frightening.

简萍：太可怕了！
Tai kěpà le!

甘玲：是啊，刚才差点儿被那只疯狗咬到。
Shì a, gāngcái chàdiǎnr bèi nà zhī fēnggǒu yǎodào.

简萍：真吓人。
Zhēn xiàrén.

Jian Ping: It is horrible!
Gan Ling: Yes, we were nearly bitten by the mad dog just now.
Jian Ping: It's scary.

T 13 太难过了。 Tài nánguò le.

I'm so sad./ I'm so upset.

① 表达痛苦、难过的心情。

Used to express the sadness or pain.

小刘：太难过了。
Tài nánguò le.

小韩：我也是，他昨天还好好儿的，今天一下子就没了（去世了）。
Wǒ yě shì, tā zuótiān hái hǎohaor de, jīntiān yīxiàzi jiù méi le（qùshì le）.

Xiao Liu: I'm so sad.

Xiao Han: Me too. He was fine yesterday, but today he's just gone(passed away).

② 叹生活困难，不易度过，表示生活状况不好。

Used to complain life is hard.

小刘：太难过了。
Tài nánguò le.

小韩：是挺难的。
Shì tǐng nán de.

小刘：唉，房贷没还完，家里的老人又生病住院。
Ài, fángdài méi huán wán, jiāli de lǎorén yòu shēngbìng zhùyuàn.

Xiao Liu: I'm so upset.
Xiao Han: It's a hard time for us.
Xian Liu: Alas, I haven't paid off the loan of the house. To make it worse my parent is in hospital now.

T 14 天气不错。Tiānqì bùcuò.

It's a nice day.

认为天气状况比较好。
Used to comment the weather is fine.

约翰：天气不错。
Tiānqì bù cuò.
杰克：是啊，我们爬白云山去吧。
Shì a, wǒmen pá Báiyún Shān qù ba.
约翰：好啊，走吧。
Hǎo a, zǒu ba.
John: It's a nice day.
Jack: Yes, how about climbing the Baiyun Mountain?
John: Good idea, let's go.

T 15 天气真好。 Tiānqì zhēn hǎo.

What a nice day.

对好的天气状况表示赞叹。
Used to express one's happiness becausr of the good weather.

徐小姐：天气真好。
Tiānqì zhēn hǎo.
黄小姐：阳光明媚，太舒服了！
Yángguāng míngmèi, tài shūfu le!
Miss Xu: What a nice day!
Miss Huang: The sun is shining brightly It is just so comfortable!

T 16 跳舞去吧。 Tiàowǔ qù ba.

Let's go dancing.

提议去跳舞。

Used to suggest going to dance.

杰克：跳舞去吧。
Tiàowǔ qù ba.

约翰：你去吧，我的脚扭伤了。
Nǐ qù ba, wǒ de jiǎo niǔshāng le.

杰克：我一个人去怪没意思的，我也不去了。
Wǒ yī gè rén qù guài méi yìsi de, wǒ yě bù qù le.

Jack: Let's go dancing.
John: You can just go by yourself. I broke my foot.
Jack: It's boring if I go there alone. Then I won't go, either.

T 17 同不同意？ Tóng bu tóngyì?

Do you agree?

询问对方同意还是不同意，表示征求对方的意见。

Used to seek for opinions by asking someone whether he /she agrees.

杰克：同不同意?
Tóng bu tóngyì?

林海：同意，真巧，我也是这么想的。
Tóngyì, zhēn qiǎo, wǒ yě shì zhème xiǎng de.

Jack: Do you agree?
Lin Hai: Yes. What a coincidence! That's just what I thought.

T 18 头有点(儿)晕。
Tóu yóudiǎnr yūn.

I feel dizzy.

① 表示头脑发昏。
To express one feels dizzy.

徐小姐：头有点（儿）晕。
Tóu yǒudiǎnr yūn.

黄小姐：怎么了?
Zěnme le?

徐小姐：感冒了。
Gǎnmào le.

Miss Xu: I feel dizzy.
Miss Huang: What's the matter with you?
Miss Xu: I caught a cold.

② 表示头脑昏乱。

To express one is too tired to think of anything.

简萍：头有点（儿）晕。
Tóu yǒudiǎnr yūn.

妈妈：该休息一会儿了，你都学习一天了。
Gāi xiūxi yīhuìr le, nǐ dōu xuéxí yī tiān le.

简萍：嗯，我睡会儿。
Ǹ, wǒ shuìhuìr.

Jian Ping: I feel dizzy.
Mum: It's time to have a break. You have been studying all day long.
Jian Ping: Yes. I go to sleep for a while.

W 1 哇，乱死了。 Wā, luànsǐ le.

Oh, what a mess.

① 叹场面或食物混乱、没有秩序。

To describe the chaos / messiness of the scenes or food, which are in disorder.

简萍：哇，乱死了。
Wā, luànsǐ le.

甘玲：是啊，房间里怎么乱成这样。
Shì a, fángjiān li zěnme luànchéng zhèyàng.

黄红：小偷把房间翻成这样了。
Xiǎotōu bǎ fángjiān fānchéng zhè yàng le.

Jian Ping: Oh, what a mess!
Gan Ling: Yes. Why is our room such a mess?
Huang Hong: Burglars must have broken in & turned the house upside down.

② 表示内心混乱，不能够做出决定或选择。

To express the confusion of one's mind for which it's hard for one to make a decision.

甘玲：哇，乱死了。
Wā, luànsǐ le.

甘玲：脑子里乱极了，我真不知道怎样才好。
Nǎozi li luànjí le, wǒ zhēn bù zhīdao zěnyàng cái hǎo.

黄红：别急，考虑好再做选择。
Bié jí, kǎolǜ hǎo zài zuò xuǎnzé.

Gan Ling: Oh, It's so confusing.
Gan Ling: I am totally confused. I really don't know what to do.
Huang Hong: Don't worry. Take it easy.

W 2 味（儿）怎么样？ Wèir zhěnmeyàng?

How about the taste?

询问食物的味道、滋味怎么样。

Used to inquire about what the taste of food is like.

约翰：味（儿）怎么样？
Wèir zěnmeyàng?

杰克：很鲜，好吃极了。
Hěn xiān, hǎochī jí le.

John: How about the taste?
Jack: That's good!

W 3 位置不错。 Wèizhì bù cuò.

Nice location!

表示物体所在的具体地点合适。

Used to show the speaker thinks the location of something is good.

黄小姐：位置不错！
Wèizhì bù cuò！

徐小姐：是啊，这里交通和购物都特方便。
Shì a, zhèli jiāoitōng hé gòuiwù dōu tè fāngibiàn.

Miss Huang: Nice location!
Miss Xu: Yes, it is very convenient for transportation and shopping.

W 4 我不怨她。
Wǒ bù yuàn tā.

I don't blame on her.

表示不怨恨带给自己麻烦或伤害的人。
To mean one doesn't bear hatred toward someone who has caused trouble and hurt to him/her.

简萍：我不怨她。
Wǒ bù yuàn tā.
甘玲：她真的太过分了。
Tā zhēn de tài guòfèn le.
简萍：这样做可能有她的难处吧。
Zhè yàng zuò kěnéng yǒu tā de nánchu ba.

Jian Ping: I don't blame on her.
Gan Ling: She's really going too far.
Jian Ping: Maybe she had her reasons for doing so.

W 5 我吃饱了。Wǒ chībǎo le.

I have had enough.

义同“我饱了”。
Used to express the same meaning as "I'm full."

W 6 我出汗了。Wǒ chūhàn le.

I am sweating.

皮肤表面已经有汗液排除，一般表示气温高或运动已经有一定的强度了。
Used to tell the listener one is sweating because of the high temperature or one's having had certain exercise.

徐小姐：我出汗了。
Wǒ chūhàn le.
黄小姐：给你纸巾，擦擦汗。
Gěi nǐ zhǐjīn, cāca hàn.

Miss Xu: I am sweating.
Miss Huang: Here's some tissue. Wipe the sweat off.

W 7 我辞职了。
Wǒ cízhí le.

I quit the job.

表示自己已经主动离开了原有的职务或工作。
Used to mean that one has resigned from previous post or job.

小刘：我辞职了。
Wǒ cízhí le.
小韩：有什么打算？
Yǒu shénme dǎsuàn?
小刘：想休息一段时间再做打算。
Xiǎng xiūxi yī duàn shíjiān zài zuò dǎsuan.

Xiao Liu: I quit the job.
Xiao Han: Do you have any new plan?
Xiao Liu: I want to have a rest before making any new plan.

W 8 我挂内科。Wǒ guà nèikē.

I want to register the internal medicine.

在医院挂号时，表示需要挂内科的号。

Used in the hospital to express one wants to register in department of the internal medicine.

病人：我挂内科。
Wǒ guà nèikē.

挂号员：好的，是普通号还是专家号？
Hǎo de, shì pǔtōnghào háishì zhuānjiāhào.

病人：普通号。
Pǔtōnghào.

Patient: I want to register the internal medicine.

Register: Ok, do you want to see a specialist or an ordinary doctor?

Patient: Ordinary.

一个音节的句子 One-syllable Sentences
两个音节的句子 Two-syllable Sentences
三个音节的句子 Three-syllable Sentences
四个音节的句子 Four-syllable Sentences

W 9 我叫你跑。 Wǒ jiào nǐ pǎo.

How dare you run away?

责斥对方不该逃跑，一般用在抓住对方时。

Used to blame someone for running away.

林海：我叫你跑！
Wǒ jiào nǐ pǎo！

小偷：……
……

林海：（抓住小偷了。）你跑啊，怎么不跑了？
（Zhuāzhù Xiǎotōu le.） Nǐ pǎo a, zěnme bù pǎo le.

Lin Hai: How dare you run away?
Thief: …
Lin Hai: (Having caught the thief.) Why didn't you run now?

② 要求对方的行为方式为跑步。

Used to urge someone to run.

林　海：我叫你跑。
Wǒ jiào nǐ pǎo.

丁小宁：我跑不动了，让我停下来歇歇吧，太累了。

Wǒ pǎo bu dòng le, ràng wǒ tíng xiàlái xiēxie ba, tài lèi le.

林　海：再不跑就来不及了。

Zài bù pǎo jiù láibují le.

Lin Hai: I told you to run.

Ding Xiaoning: I can't run any farther at all. Please let me have a break, I am too tired to move.

Lin Hai: We will be late if we don't run quickly.

W10 我叫约翰。 Wǒ jiào Yuéhàn.

I'm John.

介绍自己的名字是约翰。

Used to tell the listener his name is John.

约翰：我叫约翰。

Wǒ jiào Yuēhàn.

林海：我叫林海，认识你很高兴。

Wǒ jiào Lín Hǎi, rènshi nǐ hěn gāoxìng.

John: I'm John.

Lin Hai: I'm Lin Hai. Nice to meet you.

W11 我来晚了。
Wǒ lái wǎn le.

I'm sorry I'm late.

① 因迟到表示歉意。
Used to make apology for being late.

徐小姐：我来晚了。
Wǒ lái wǎn le.

黄小姐：没关系。
Méi guānxi.

徐小姐：让你们等这么久，真不好意思。
Ràng nǐmen děng zhème jiǔ, zhēn bùhǎo yìsi.

Miss Xu: I'm sorry I'm late.
Miss Huang: Never mind.
Miss Xu: I am sorry for having kept you waiting for such a long time.

② 因迟到表示遗憾。
Used to show one's pity for being late.

徐小姐：我来晚了。
Wǒ lái wǎn le.

黄小姐：刚开始，开场挺精彩的。
Gāng kāishǐ, kāichǎng tǐng jīngcǎi de.

徐小姐：唉，错过了，真可惜！
Ài, cuòguò le, zhēn kěxī!

Miss Xu: I'm sorry I'm late.
Miss Huang: It started just a moment ago. The opening show is excellent.
Miss Xu: Alas, I missed the excellent opening ceremony. What a pity!

W12 我买些梨。Wǒ mǎi xiē lí.

I want to buy some pears.

在水果店、商场或超市，告诉售货员自己想买的水果是梨。

Used in the fruit store, shopping center or supermarket to tell the assistant that one wants to buy some pears.

约　翰：我买些梨。
Wǒ mǎixiē lí.

售货员：你自己挑（挑选）。
Nǐ zìji tiāo（tiāoxuǎn）.

约　翰：好的，谢谢。
Hǎo de, xièxie.

John: I want to buy some pears.
Assistant: You can pick out some pears by yourself.
John: OK. Thanks.

W13 我们谈谈。 Wǒmen tántan.

Let's have a talk.

提议双方就相关问题进行讨论。
Used to suggest a talk between the speaker & the listener.

林海：我们谈谈。
Wǒmen tántan.
简萍：还谈什么呢？
Hái tán shénme ne?
林海：我想解释一下上午发生的事。
Wǒ xiǎng jiěshì yīxià shàngwǔ fāshēng de shì.

Lin Hai: Let's have a talk.
Jian Ping: What's the point of talking any more?
Lin Hai: I want to explain to you what happened this morning.

W14 我们走吧。
Wǒmen zǒu ba.

Let's go.

提议或催促对方前往或离开某地。

Used to advise or urge someone to leave a place or to leave for some place.

约翰：我们走吧。
Wǒmen zǒu ba.

杰克：急什么，再坐会儿。
Jí shénme, zài zuòhuìr.

约翰：再不走就迟到了。
Zài bù zǒu jiù chídào le.

John: Let's go.

Jack: Don't worry. Let's stay here for a while.

John: Or we will be late.

W15 我认识他/她。
Wǒ rènshi tā.

I know him/her.

告诉对方自己认识某人。

Used to tell someone you know that person.

约翰：我认识她。
Wǒ rènshi tā.
杰克：那位小姐吗?
Nà wèi xiǎojie ma?
约翰：是的，她是林海的妹妹林欣。
Shì de, tā shì Lín Hǎi de mèimei lín Xīn.

John: I know her.
Jack: That lady?
John: Yes, she is Lin Xin, Lin Hai's sister.

W16 我洗个澡。 Wǒ xǐ gè zǎo.

I'm going to take a shower.

表示自己想去洗澡。

Used to express one wants to take a shower.

丈夫：我洗个澡。
Wǒ xǐ gè zǎo.
妻子：去吧，热水已经放好了。
Qù ba, rèshuǐ yǐjīng fànghǎo le.

Husband: I'm going to take a shower.
Wife: OK. I have prepared water for you in the bathtub.

W17 我想喝水。

Wǒ xiǎng hē shuǐ.

I want to drink some water.

表示自己口渴希望喝水。

Used to tell others one is thirsty and want to have some water.

女儿：我想喝水。
　　　Wǒ xiǎng hē shuǐ.

妈妈：杯子里有凉的，去喝吧。
　　　Bēizi li yǒu liáng de, qù hē ba.

女儿：谢谢妈妈。
　　　Xièxie māma.

Daughter: I want to drink some water.

Mum: There is some cool boiled water in the cup. Go to have it.

Daughter: Thanks, Mum.

W18 我想家了。

Wǒ xiǎng jiā le.

I am homesick.

表示自己思念家乡和亲人。

Used to express one misses one's families.

约翰：我想家了。
Wǒ xiǎng jiā le.
杰克：是啊，我们来中国都一年多了，我也想家了。
Shì a, wǒmen lái Zhōngguó dōu yī nián duō le, wǒ yě xiǎng jiā le.
John: I am homesick.
Jack: Yes, me too. We have been in China for more than a year.

W19 我想睡了。
Wǒ xiǎng shuì le.

I want to sleep/I’m going to bed.

表示自己希望睡觉了。
Used to tell the listener you hope to go to sleep.

女儿：我想睡了。
Wǒ xiǎng shuì le.
妈妈：不早了，去睡吧。
Bù zǎo le, qù shuì ba.
Daughter: I want to sleep./I’m going to bed.
Mum: It’s getting late. Go to bed.

W20 我要退房。Wǒ yào tuìfáng.

I would like to return the house to you./ I would like to check out.

① 表示希望退还给售房机构已经购买的房子。

Used to express one wants to return the house to the real estate company.

徐小姐：我要退房。
Wǒ yào tuìfáng.
售房小姐：这个恐怕不行。
Zhè gè kǒngpà bùxíng.

Miss Xu: I would like to return the house to you.
Salesman: I am afraid you can't.

② 在酒店或旅馆前台，对服务员表示自己结束住宿，需要办理退宿手续。

Used to express one needs to check out at the reception desk in a hotel.

黄小姐：我要退房。
Wǒ yào tuìfáng.

前台服务员：好的，您住几号房？
Hǎo de, nín zhù jǐ hào fáng?
黄小姐：2栋，1022房。
2 dòng, 1022 fáng.

Miss Huang: I would like to check out.
Receptionist: OK. Which room did you stay in?
Miss Huang: Room 1022, Building 2.

W21 我想退货。
Wǒ xiǎng tuìhuò.

I would like to return the goods.

向商家表示自己想退还所购买的物品。
Used to show you want to return the goods to the seller.

顾　客：我想退货。
Wǒ xiǎng tuìhuò.
售货员：请你到总服务台去办理，这里不办理退货业务。
Qǐng nǐ dào zǒng fúwùtái qù bànlǐ, zhèli bù bànlǐ tuìhuò yèwù.
顾　客：谢谢。
Xièxie.

Customer: I would like to return the goods.
Salesman: Please go to the front desk. We are not in charge of returned goods.

W22 我有点儿冷。 Wǒ yǒudiǎnr lěng.

I feel cold.

表示感觉温度偏低。

Used to mean that the temperature is low and one feels cold.

女儿：我有点儿冷。
Wǒ yǒudiǎnr lěng.

妈妈：今天降温了，再加件衣服。
Jīntiān jiàngwēn le, zài jiā jiàn yīfu.

Daughter: I feel cold.
Mum: Today the temperature gets lower, So put on more clothes.

W23 我再试试。Wǒ zài shìshi.

I will try it again.

打算再次尝试。

Used to mean one is going to try something again.

黄红：我再试试。
Wǒ zài shìshi.
甘玲：瓶盖儿拧得太紧了，要不，找个男生帮忙开。
Pínggàir nǐng de tài jǐn le, yàobù, zhǎo gè nánshēng bāngmáng kāi.
黄红：我试试再说吧。
Wǒ shìshi zài shuō ba.

Huang Hong: I will try it again.
Gan Ling: The bottle cap is too tight. How about asking a boy for help.
Huang Hong: Let me try again. Yes! It opens finally!

W24 我真糊涂。Wǒ zhēn hútu.

What an idiot I am!

责怪自己不明事理做了不该做的的事情或者说了不该说的话。

Used to blame oneself for having done or said something unreasonable.

约翰：我真糊涂。
Wǒ zhēn hútu.

杰克：怎么了？
Zěnme le?

约翰：我把上午听讲座的事记成了下午，真可惜，错过了一次重要的讲座。
Wǒ bǎ shàngwǔ tīng jiǎngzuò de shì jìchéng le xiàwǔ, zhēn kěxī, cuò guò le yī cì zhòngyào de jiǎngzuò.

John: What an idiot I am!

Jack: What's up?

John: I thought the lecture was in the afternoon instead of in the morning. What a pity! I have missed an important lecture.

W25 我租套房。
Wǒ zhū tào fáng.

I want to rent an apartment.

表示希望租用房屋。

Used to express someone wants to rent a house.

徐小姐：我租套房。
Wǒ zū tào fáng.

房屋中介：你要什么样的房子?
Nǐ yào shénmeyàng de fángzǐ?

徐小姐：我想租小两房一厅的。
Wǒ xiǎng zū xiǎo liǎng fáng yī tīng de.

Miss Xu: I want to rent an apartment.

Agent: What kind of apartment do you want?

Miss Xu: I would like to rent an apartment with two bedrooms and a living room.

W26 雾太大了。 Wù tài dà le.

The fog is heavy.

表示雾气很大。

Used to explain the fog is dense/heavy.

小刘：雾太大了。
Wù tài dà le.

小韩：是啊，前面20米就看不清了，你开车小心点儿。
Shì a, qiánmiàn 20 mǐ jiù kànbuqīng le, nǐ kāichē xiǎoxīndiǎnr.

Xiao Liu: The fog is heavy.

Xiao Han: Yes, we can't see the thing 20 meters away, Be careful when you are drive.

X 1 喜欢哪款? Xǐhuan nǎ kuǎn?

Which one do you like?

询问喜爱哪个款式的物品。

Used to inquire which design one likes.

爸爸：喜欢哪款？
Xǐhuan nǎ kuǎn?
女儿：Iphone5。
Iphone5.
爸爸：那就买这款。
Nà jiù mǎi zhè kuǎn.
女儿：谢谢爸爸。
Xièxie bàba.

Dad: Which one do you like?
Daughter: Iphone 5.
Dad: OK, let's take this one.
Daughter: Thanks, Daddy!

X 2 下午有雨。
Xiǎwǔ yǒu yǔ.

It's going to rain this afternoon.

推测或预报下午会下雨。
Used to predict it is going to rain this afternoon.

林　海：下午有雨。
Xiàwǔ yǒu yǔ.
丁小宁：那下午的篮球赛怎么办？
Nà xiàwǔ de lánqiú sài zěnme bàn?
林　海：继续呀。天气预报这么说，还不知道准不准呢。

Jìxù ya. tiānqì yùbào zhème shuō, hái bù zhīdao zhǔnbu zhǔn ne.

丁小宁：就是下雨也没关系。

Jiùshì xiàyǔ yě méi guānxi.

Lin Hai: It's going to rain this afternoon.

Ding Xiaoning: Shall we have the basketball match then?

Lin Hai: Sure. Weather forecast just says so , but it may not rain.

Ding Xiaoning: It doesn't matter even if it rians.

X 3 现在几点? Xiànzài jǐ diǎn?

What time is it now?

义同"几点了"。

Used to express the same meaning as "几点了".

X4 现在几月？ Xiànzài jǐ yuè?

What month is it?

询问当前的月份。
Used to inquire which month it is.

小刘：现在几月？
Xiànzài jǐ yuè?
小韩：三月。
Sān yuè.

Xiao Liu: What month is it?
Xiao Han: March.

X5 谢谢捧场。 Xièxie pěngchǎng.

Thanks for your attendance/support.

对特意到活动现场予以支持的人表示感谢。
Used to express one's gratitude to the supporters.

徐小姐：谢谢捧场！
Xièxie pěngchǎng！

小　韩：甭客气。
Béng kèqi.

Miss Xu: Thanks for your attendance/ support.

Xiao Han: You're welcome.

X 6 行啦，走吧。
Xíng la, zǒu ba.

Well, let's go!

表示可以走了，催促对方离开。

Used to urge people to leave.

林　海：行啦，走吧。
Xíng la , zǒu ba.

丁小宁：过山车真刺激，我想再坐一次。
Guòshānchē zhēn cìjī, wǒ xiǎng zài zuò yī cì.

林　海：你还没完没了啦，走吧，我们玩其它的。
Nǐ hái méi wán méi liǎo la, zǒu ba, wǒmen wán qítā de.

丁小宁：好吧。
Hǎo bā.

Lin Hai:]Well, let's go!

Ding Xiaoning: The roller coaster is very exciting. I want to play it again.
Lin Hai: Can't you finish with it? Let's go and play other games!
Ding Xiaoning: OK.

X 7 行李车呢？ Xínglichē ne?

Where is the luggage cart?

询问行李车在哪里。

Used to inquire where the luggage cart is.

约翰：行李车呢？
　　Xíngli chē ne?
杰克：在那里呢，我这就去推。
　　Zài nàli ne, wǒ zhè jiù qù tuī.

John: Where is the luggage cart?
Jack: It's over there. I go to get it.

Y 1 一路顺风。 Yī lù shùnfēng.

Have a nice trip!

祝愿出行的人一路顺利、平安。

Used to wish a traveler to have a good trip

林　海：一路顺风！
　　　　Yī lù shùnfēng！

丁小宁：谢谢。
　　　　Xièxie.

Lin Hai: Have a nice trip!
Ding Xiaoning: Thank you!

Y 2 一起走吧。 Yīqǐ zǒu ba.

Let's go together!

提议对方同自己一起走。

Used to advise another person to go with you.

黄红：一起走吧。
　　　Yīqǐ zǒu ba.

简萍：我还有事，你先走吧。
Wǒ hái yǒu shì, nǐ xiān zǒu ba.
Huang Hong: Let's go together!
Jian Ping: I have something to deal with. You go first.

Y 3 要忌口吗？ Yào jìkǒu ma?

Is there anything I can't eat?

询问有没有不能吃的食物。（“忌口”，因生病或其他原因不适宜吃某些食物。）

Used to inquire whether there is anything one can't eat. “忌口” means one must avoid eating something because of illness or other reasons.

小韩：要忌口吗？
Yào jìkǒu ma?
小刘：血糖高，不能吃甜食。
Xuètáng gāo, bùnéng chī tiánshí.
Xiao Han: Is there anything I can't eat?
Xiao Liu: You can't eat sweet food because of high blood sugar.

Y 4 要些小吃？ Yào xiē xiǎochī?

Do you want some snack?

① 询问是否需要一些分量小、价钱低的简单菜肴果品。

Used to inquire whether you need small portion and cheaper dish or fruit.

徐小姐：要些小吃？
Yào xiē xiǎochī?

小　刘：好哇。
Hǎo wa.

徐小姐：靓女，来两碟凤爪、花生。
Liàngnǚ, lái liǎng dié fèngzhǎo、huāshēng.

Miss Xu: Do you want some snack?
Xiao Liu: OK!
Miss Xu: Waitress，Two dishes of chicken feet and peanuts, please.

② 询问是否需要一些风味食品（如春卷、年糕、粽子等）。

Used to inquire whether one needs some typical local food (such as spring roll, rice cake, zongzi and the like).

徐小姐：要些小吃？
Yào xiē xiǎochi?
黄小姐：好哇，这里的特色食品是春卷。
Hǎo wa, zhèli de tèsè shípǐn shì chūnjuǎn.
徐小姐：靓女，来碟春卷。
Liàngnǚ, lái dié chūnjuǎn.

Miss Xu: Do you want some snacks?
Miss Huang: OK! Spring roll is typical local food.
Miss Xu: Waitress,a plate of Spring Roll, please.

Y 5 要预约吗？
Yào yùyuē ma?

Do I need to make an appointment?

询问是否需要事先约定。
Used to inquire whether one needs to have an appointment.

小刘：要预约吗？
Yào yùyuē ma?
小韩：当然，广州酒家可火了，需要提前一天预约才能订到位。
Dāngrán, Guǎngzhōu Jiǔjiā kě huǒ le, xūyào tíqián yī tiān yùyuē cái néng dìngdào wèi.

小刘：我马上打电话预约。
Wǒ mǎshàng dǎ diànhuà yùyuē.

Xiao Liu: Do I need to make an appointment?
Xiao Han: Sure! Guangzhou Restaurant is very popular and you need to make an appointment 2 days in advance.
Xiao liu: I will call to make an appointment right now.

Y 6 音乐太响。
Yīnyuè tài xiǎng.

The music is too loud.

认为音乐的音量太大。
Used to complain the volume of the music is too high.

甘　玲：音乐太响。
Yīnyuè tài xiǎng.
丁小宁：我把声音调小点儿。
Wǒ bǎ shēngyīn tiáo xiǎodiǎnr.

Gan Ling: The Music is too loud.
Ding Xiaoning: I'll turn the volume down.

Y 7 有班车吗?
Yǒu bānchē ma?

Do you have a shuttle bus?

询问是否有按固定线路、固定时间行驶的客车。

Used to inquire whether there is a bus coming and going regularly.

甘玲：有班车吗?
Yǒu bānchē ma?
林海：有，15分钟一班。
Yǒu, 15 fēnzhōng yī bān.

Gan Ling: Do you have shuttle bus?
Lin Hai: Yes, there is one every 15 minutes.

Y 8 有车位吗?
Yǒu chēwèi ma?

Do you have a place for parking?

询问是否有停车的位置。

Used to inquire whether there is a parking place.

小韩：有车位吗？
Yǒu chēwèi ma?
停车场管理员：没有了，你到前面那个停车场看看。
Méiyǒu le, nǐ dào qiánmiàn nà gè tíngchēchǎng kànkan.
小韩：谢谢。
Xièxie.

Xiao Han: Do you have a place for parking?
Parking administrator: No, You can go to the parking lot over there.
Xiao Han: Thanks.

Y 9 有地图吗？ Yǒu dìtú ma?

Do you have a map/maps to sell?

① 询问是否有地图出售。
Used to inquire whether one has a map for sale.

小　韩：有地图吗？
Yǒu dìtú ma?
售货员：有。有两种，一种是标有具体景点的，一种是标有酒店位置的，你要哪种?
Yǒu. yǒu liǎng zhǒng, yī zhǒng shì biāo yǒu jùtǐ jǐngdiǎn de, yī zhǒng shì biāo yǒu jiǔdiàn wèizhì de, nǐ yào nǎ zhǒng?

小　韩：我要标有具体景点的。
wǒ yào biāo yǒu jùtǐ jǐngdiǎn de.

Xiao Han: Do you have maps to sell?
Salesman: Yes, there are two kinds. One is for scene spots and the other is for hotels.

② 询问对方是否有地图，表示需要地图。

Used to inquire whether someone has got a map ,which means one needs it.

林　海：有地图吗?
Yǒu dìtú ma?

丁小宁：有，就在我书桌的抽屉里，你自己拿。
Yǒu, jiù zài wǒ shūzhuō de chōu tili, nǐ zìjǐ ná.

林　海：好的。
Hǎo de.

Lin Hai: Do you have a map?
Ding Xiaoning: Yes, it's in the drawer of my desk. Go and fetch it.

Y 10 有电梯吗？ Yǒu diàntī ma?

Is there a lift?

询问楼宇等建筑物中是否配有电梯。

Used to inquire whether there is a lift in a building.

徐小姐：有电梯吗？
Yǒu diàntī ma?

房屋中介：是老房子，没有电梯。
Shì lǎo fángzi, méiyǒu diàntī.

徐小姐：那就算了，谢谢。
Nà jiù suàn le, xièxie.

Miss Xu: Is there a lift?
Agent: No, It is an old building.
Miss Xu: Then let me turn to other buildings Thanks!

Y 11 有啤酒吗？ Yǒu píjiǔ ma?

Do you have beer?

① 询问是否有啤酒出售，表示想购买啤酒。

Used to inquire whether there is beer for sale.

小　韩：有啤酒吗?
Yǒu píjiǔ ma?
售货员：有，要什么牌子的?
Yǒu, yào shénme páizi de?
小　韩：珠江啤酒。
Zhūjiāng píjiǔ.

Xiao Han: Do you have beer?
Salesman: Yes, which brand do you want?
Xiao Han: Zhu Jiang beer.

② 询问是否存有啤酒，表示想喝啤酒。

Used to inquire whether there is beer, meaning one wants to have a drink.

小刘：有啤酒吗?
Yǒu píjiǔ ma?
小韩：冰箱里有，自己拿。
Bīngxiāng li yǒu, zìji ná.
小刘：我今天要喝个痛快。
Wǒ jīntiān yào hē gè tòngkuài.

Xiao Liu: Do you have beer?
Xiao Han: It's in the refrigerator. Go to fetch it by yourself.
Xiao Liu: I am going to drink to my heart's content today!

Y 12 有字幕吗？ Yǒu zìmù ma?

Does it have subtitles?

询问电影银幕、电视屏幕或舞台的某个位置（下边或旁边）是否配有文字。

Used to inquire whether there are subtitles in a film.

小刘：有字幕吗？
Yǒu zìmù ma?
小韩：有中文字幕。
Yǒu zhōngwén zìmù.

Xiao Liu: Does it have subtitles?
Xiao Han: Yes, it has Chinese subtitles.

Y 13 又咳嗽了。 Yòu késou le.

You/I have a coughing again.

表示反复地咳嗽。

Used to express one has a cough again.

一个音节的句子 One-syllable Sentences
两个音节的句子 Two-syllable Sentences
三个音节的句子 Three-syllable Sentences
四个音节的句子 Four-syllable Sentences

徐小姐：又咳嗽了。
Yòu késou le.
黄小姐：是啊，我都咳嗽好几天了。
Shì a, wǒ dōu késou hǎo jǐ tiān le.

Miss Xu: You have a coughing again.
Miss Huang: Yes, it has lasted for a few days.

Y 14 又晚点了。
Yǒu wǎndiǎn le.

It's behind schedule again.

表示车（船或飞机）发出或到达经常比规定时间晚。
Used to express the ship or plane arrives frequently later than the schedule time.

甘玲：又晚点了。
Yòu wǎndiǎn le.
黄红：都习惯了，这趟班车经常晚点。
Dōu xíguàn le, zhè tàng bānchē jīngcháng wǎndiǎn.

Gan Ling: It's behind schedule again.
Huang Hong: I've got used to it . This train is often late.

Y 15 鱼新鲜吗？

Yú xīnxian ma?

Is the fish fresh?

询问鱼是否变质。

Used to inquire whether the fish has gone bad.

徐小姐：鱼新鲜吗？
　　　　Yú xīnxian ma?

鱼贩子：新鲜，刚才还是活的。
　　　　Xīnxian, gāngcái háishì huó de.

徐小姐：我要这条。
　　　　Wǒ yào zhè tiáo.

Miss Xu: Is the fish fresh?
Salesman: Yes, it was alive just now.
Miss Xu: Ok.I take this one.

Z 1 在哪（儿）买的？ Zài nǎr mǎi de?

Where did you buy it?

询问购买某件商品的地点。

Used to ask someone where he/she bought a good.

徐小姐：在哪（儿）买的？
　　　　Zài nǎr mǎi de?
黄小姐：楼下的超市。
　　　　Lóuxià de chāoshì.

Miss Xu: Where did you buy it?
Miss Huang: In the supermarket downstairs.

Z 2 在哪（儿）拍的？ Zài nǎr pāi de?

Where did you take the photo?

① 询问照片在什么地方拍摄的。

Used to ask the place where the photo was taken.

甘玲：在哪（儿）拍的？
　　　Zài nǎr pāi de?

黄红：桂林，暑假在桂林拍的，好看吧。
Guìlín, shǔjià zài Guìlín pāi de, hǎo kàn ba.

甘玲：很好看。
Hěnhǎo kàn.

Gan Ling: Where did you take the photo?
Huang Hong: I took it in Guilin this summer holiday.
Gan Ling: It looks beautiful!

② 问商品在哪个网站上购买的。

Used to ask on which online store one has bought the goods.

甘玲：在哪（儿）拍的?
Zài nǎr pāi de?

简萍：淘宝上拍的，又便宜又漂亮。
Táobǎo shàng pāi de, yòu piányi yòu piāoliang.

甘玲：我也去拍一件。
Wǒ yě qù pāi yī jiàn.

Gan Ling: On which online store did you buy the goods?
Jian Ping: On Taobao.
Gan Ling: I will buy one there.

Z 3 在哪（儿）停车？
Zài nǎr tíngche?

Where is parking lot?

询问汽车停在什么地方。

Used to inquire where the parking place is.

小刘：在哪（儿）停车？
　　Zài nǎr tíngchē?
小韩：就在前面超市附近。
　　Jiù zài qiánmiàn chāoshì fùjìn.

Xiao Liu: Where is the parking lot?
Xiao Han: It's near that supermarket.

Z 4 怎么回事？
Zěnme huíshì?

What's wrong?

询问发生了什么事情。

Used to ask what has happened.

林　海：怎么回事？
　　Zěnme huí shì?

丁小宁：大概又跳闸了。
Dàgài yòu tiàozhá le.
林　海：到处黑乎乎的，得赶紧修哇。
Dàochǔ hēihūhū de, děi gǎnjǐn xiū wa.

Lin Hai: What's wrong?
Ding Xiaoling: It has tripped.
Lin Hai: It's dark everywhere and let's fix it immediately.

Z 5 怎么样啊？ Zěnmeyàng a?

How is it going ?

询问事情的结果。

Used to ask what the result is.

徐小姐：怎么样啊？
Zěnmeyàng a?
小　刘：还在手术中，情况还不清楚。
Hái zài shǒushù zhōng, qíngkuàng hái bù qīngchu.

Miss Xu: How is it going ?
Xiao Liu: The operation is still on and we are not clear about it yet.

Z 6 找我有事？

Zhǎo wǒ yǒu shì?

Are you looking for me?

① 想确认要找的人是不是我。

Used to make sure whether someone wants to find the speaker himself.

小刘：找我有事？
Zhǎo wǒ yǒu shì?
徐小姐：对啊。
Duì a.

Xiao Liu: Are you looking for me?
Miss Xu: Yes.

② 询问对方为了什么事找自己。

Used to ask for what reason someone is coming to the speaker.

徐小姐：找我有事？
Zhǎo wǒ yǒu shì?
黄小姐：是啊，最近手头儿有点紧，想找你借点儿钱。
Shì a, zuìjìn shǒutóur yǒudiǎn jǐn, xiǎng zhǎo nǐ jièdiǎnr qián.

Miss Xu: For what are you looking for me?
Miss Huang: I am short of money recently, so I want to borrow some money from you.

Z 7 这么多人。Zhème duō rén.

There are so many people.

人数超过了预计的数目，表示人很多。

Used to express the number of people is beyond the estimated one.

甘　玲：这么多人！
Zhème duō rén!

丁小宁：没想到来这么多同学。
Méi xiǎng dào lái zhème duō tóngxué.

甘　玲：怎么办，我们准备的资料恐怕不够。
Zěnme bàn, wǒ men zhǔnbèi de zīliào kǒngpà bù gòu.

丁小宁：现在也来不及印，只能有多少发多少啦。
Xiànzài yě láibùjí yìn, zhǐnéng yǒu duōshao fā duōshao la.

Gan Ling: There are so many people.
Ding Xiaoning: I didn't expect so many classmates would come.
Gan Ling: I am afraid that the material we've prepared is not enough.
Ding Xiaoning: We don't have time to prepare more. Just hand out as many as we have.

一个音节的句子 One-syllable Sentences
两个音节的句子 Two-syllable Sentences
三个音节的句子 Three-syllable Sentences
四个音节的句子 Four-syllable Sentences

Z 8 这儿真舒服。
Zhèr zhēn shūfu.

It's comfortable here.

表示所处的地方让人感到轻松愉快。

Used to praise a place which is comfortable.

甘玲：这儿真舒服。
Zhèr zhēn shūfu.
黄红：是啊，这里的空气都是甜的。
Shì a, zhèli de kōngqì dōu shì tián de.

Gan Ling: It's comfortable here.
Huang Hong: Yes, the air is pure and sweet here.

Z 9 真不容易！
Zhēn bù róngyi!

It's difficult!

① 感叹做某些事情很艰难。

Used to exclaim it's difficult to deal

with some things.

小刘：真不容易！
Zhēn bù róngyi！

小韩：是啊，为了给孩子报上名，我早上三点钟就去市少年宫排队了。
Shì a, wèile gěi háizi bàoshàng míng, wǒ zǎoshàng sān diǎn zhōng jiù qù shì shǎoniángōng páiduì le.

小刘：这么早！
Zhème zǎo！

Xiao Liu: It's difficult!

Xiao Han: Yes, I got up at 3 am to wait on line in children's palace to apply for registration for my child.

Xiao Liu: You get up so early!

Z 10 真够冷的。
Zhēn gòu lěng de.

It's terribly cold.

① 表示气温过低，让人觉得寒冷。
Used to show the temperature is so

low that one feels very cold.

甘玲：真够冷的。
Zhēn gòu lěng de.
简萍：是啊，冷得我手指头都伸不直。
Shì a, lěngde wǒ shǒuzhǐtou dōu shēn bù zhí.
Gan Ling: It's terribly cold!
Jian Pin: Yes, it's too cold to straighten my fingers.

② 表示人冷冰冰的，不热情。

Used to indicate that a person is indifferent.

小刘：真够冷的。
Zhēn gòu lěng de.
小韩：你不知道她是我们这儿的冷美人呀。
Nǐ bù zhīdao tā shì wǒmen zhèr de lěng měirén ya.
小刘：我真没见她笑过。
Wǒ zhēn méi jiàn tā xiào guo.
Xiao Liu: She is indifferent.
Xiao Han: You don't know she is called 'indifferent beauty' here.
Xiao Liu: I have never seen her smile.

Z 11 真好玩儿。Zhēn hǎowánr.

It's funny!

形容表示人或者事很有趣。

Used to describe someone or something is funny.

甘玲：真好玩儿！
Zhēn hǎowánr!

简萍：这个游戏既新鲜又刺激，我也觉得好玩儿。
Zhè gè yóuxì jì xīnxian yòu cìjī, wǒ yě juéde hǎowánr.

Gan Ling: It's funny!

Jian Ping: I think so! This game is fresh and exciting.

Z 12 周末愉快。Zhōumò yúkuài.

Have a nice weekend.

祝福语，希望对方有个愉快的周末。

Used as a blessing to wish someone to have a good weekend.

Z 13 走，唱K去。
Zǒu, zhàng K qù.

Let's go and have karaoke.

邀请对方到KTV去唱歌。
Used to invite the listener to go to sing in a karaoke.

甘玲：走，唱K去。
Zǒu, chàng K qù.
简萍：好啊，等我一下儿，换双鞋就走。
Hǎo a, děng wǒ yīxiàr, huàn shuāng xié jiù zǒu.

Gan Ling: Let's go and have karaoke.
Jian Pin: OK. Wait a moment. Let me put on another pair of shoes.

Z 14 坐这（儿）行吗？
Zuò zhèr xíng ma?

Can I sit here, please?

① 询问坐的位置是否合适。
Used to inquire whether it's suitable for one to sit in a certain position.

简萍：坐这（儿）行吗?
Zuò zhèr xíng ma?
黄红：好像有点儿近，我们往后坐点儿，这样看才舒服。
Hǎoxiàng yǒudiǎnr jìn, wǒmen wǎng hòu zuò diǎnr, zhèyàng kàn cái shūfu.

Jian Ping: Can we sit here, please?
Huang Hong: It's close to the front. It will be more comfortable if we sit a little further.

② 询问这个位置是否可以坐。

Used to inquire whether one can sit in certain seat.

林海：坐这（儿）行吗?
Zuò zhèr xíng ma?
简萍：不好意思，这个座位已经有人了。
Bùhǎoyìsi, zhè gè zuòwèi yǐjīng yǒu rén le.

Lin Hai: Can I take this seat, please?
Jian Ping: Sorry, it is occupied.

音节索引表
Syllabary

一个音节的句子
One-syllable Sentences

二个音节的句子
Two-syllable Sentences

音节索引表
Syllabary

二个音节的句子
Two-syllable Sentences

三个音节的句子
Three-syllable Sentences

四个音节的句子
Four-syllable Sentences

四个音节的句子
Four-syllable Sentences

图书在版编目（CIP）数据

汉语1234 / 刘惠琼等编著.
北京：外文出版社，2013年（轻松开始学汉语系列）
ISBN 978-7-119-07357-6

I.①汉… II.①刘… III.①汉语 – 对外汉语教学 – 自学参考资料 IV.① H195.4

中国版本图书馆CIP数据核字（2013）第085558号

选题策划 曲　径
责任编辑 曲　径
装帧设计 腾昭欣
印刷监制 冯　浩

汉语1234

作　　者 刘惠琼 主编

出版发行 外文出版社有限责任公司
地　　址 中国北京西城区百万庄大街24号
邮政编码 100037
网　　址 http://www.flp.com.cn
电子邮箱 flp@cipg.org.cn
电　　话 008610-68320579（总编室）
008610-68327750（版权部）
008610-68995852（发行部）
008610-68996075（编辑部）
印　　刷 北京和谐彩色印刷有限公司
经　　销 新华书店 / 外文书店
开　　本 787mm × 1092mm　1/48
印　　张 7.75
版　　次 2014年8月 第1版 第1次印刷
书　　号 ISBN 978-7-119-07357-6
定　　价 05900 （汉英）